THE YOUNGEST MOTHERS

To my children, Marianne and Jonathan.

The Youngest Mothers

The experience of pregnancy and motherhood
among young women of school age

GILLIAN SCHOFIELD

School of Social Work, University of East Anglia

Avebury

Aldershot • Brookfield USA • Hong Kong • Singapore • Sydney

Published by
Avebury
Ashgate Publishing Limited
Gower House
Croft Road
Aldershot
Hants GU11 3HR
England

Ashgate Publishing Company
Old Post Road
Brookfield
Vermont 05036
USA

Typeset by Neville Young
49 Muswell Avenue
London N10 2EH

British Library Cataloguing in Publication Data

Schofield, Gillian
    Youngest Mothers:
    The experience of pregnancy and motherhood among young women of school age
    I. Title
    362.8392

    ISBN 1-85628-843-9

Library of Congress Cataloging-in-Publication Data

Schofield, Gillian, 1951–
    The youngest mothers : The experience of pregnancy and motherhood among young women of school age / Gillian Schofield
        p.   cm.
    Includes bibliographical references.
    ISBN 1-85628-843-9 : $55.95 (approx.)
    1. Teenage mothers--Great Britain.   2. Pregnant schoolgirls--Great Britain.
    I. Title
    HQ759.S2754   1994
    306.874'3--dc20   94-30649
                                                                CIP

Printed and bound by Athenæum Press Ltd.,
Gateshead, Tyne & Wear.

Contents

Part I
Setting the scene: theory and research on school age pregnancy and motherhood

Part II
The experience of pregnancy, birth and motherhood:
school age mothers tell their story

Part III
Analysis of the issues: some practical implications for services

Figures and tables

Acknowledgements

I would like to thank the Ormiston Trust for giving me the opportunity to undertake this research. I have also much appreciated the patient help and support of Professor Peter Wedge and other colleagues in the School of Social Work at the University of East Anglia.

I must thank my friends, Abby and Antony Hurden, for their diligent work in producing the manuscript.

Finally and most importantly I would like to thank the young women who so willingly shared their ideas, their emotions and their wisdom. It was a privilege to meet them and to hear their story.

Preface

The importance of considering the experiences of very young mothers was confirmed in 1992 when the Government made the prevention of pregnancy under the age of 16 one of the targets set for the Health Service. In *The Health of the Nation*, the rate of conceptions under the age of 16 was targeted to be reduced by at least 50 per cent by the year 2000. (Department of Health 1992). The argument in the White Paper ran something like this. Unwanted or unintended pregnancies were seen as a sign of the nation's sexual ill-health. It was suggested that although nearly half of all pregnancies are said to be unwanted or unintended, it is difficult to collect information about such a varied group. For convenience, the Government therefore selected one particular group; all pregnancies under the age of 16 can be presumed to be unwanted. The target therefore must be to reduce those numbers by half and increasing the provision of sex education and contraceptive services for young people is proposed as the best way of tackling this.

This may seem, at a common sense level, an entirely sensible area to target and the proposal for increased provision in this area must be welcome – although it is unclear whether additional resources will be allocated for the achievement of these health targets. What, however, is noticeable about the document itself and became even more striking in the media reporting of the targets, is that pregnant fifteen year olds are grouped with people suffering from AIDS and other sexually transmitted diseases. This may be a convenient way of categorising and grouping 'problems' for society, but the underlying message to those girls, their families and the agencies responsible for providing services for them is that the pregnancy is a significant medical problem. It is not difficult to see that those young women who decide not to rid themselves of this 'illness' through abortion or adoption but choose to keep the child, risk being subjected to a range of negative images. In referring to women in general the document uses the words 'unwanted or unintended pregnancies' and the concession is made that not all of these pregnancies result in unwanted babies. Referring to younger women, only the words 'unwanted pregnancies' are used and there is no mention of the possibility that by the time of the birth, even young mothers may want their babies. Such tensions and contradictions to which very young mothers are exposed form the centre of this book.

Introduction

This research project came about initially as the result of a wish by the Ormiston Trust, a voluntary child care organisation, to consider the work of their tuition unit as a resource for pregnant school girls and school age mothers. The unit had been operating within a family centre for eight years and it was felt desirable to take stock of progress to date in order to evaluate its effectiveness and plan for the future. The impression of the staff was that contrary to the negative images around about young mothers, the young women they worked with seemed to be adapting very well to their role as mothers. So behind the question about the role of the unit there was a more general feeling of mystification about the contrast between the popular image of the school age mother and the young women they worked with on a day to day basis.

There were a number of contradictions which needed to be understood. First, there was the fact that although motherhood is highly valued in our society, there is a prescribed framework for its value; motherhood outside that framework has negative associations and can be seen as deviant. The marital status of a mother has become less a source of stigma but the age of a mother is seen as significant, not just in terms of individually deviant behaviour but as a source of social pollution.

The issue of age is therefore fundamental to this debate. As a society, we regularly set age limits as a convenient way of indicating the readiness of an individual to take on adult roles. The anomalies during the teenage years in particular are obvious; it is necessary to be older to vote than to get married, join the army and so on. It is necessary to be older to have homosexual relationships than heterosexual relationships. It is part of our culture to equate maturity with chronological age and although most would accept that there is a range of maturity at any specific age, each year group during childhood has acquired its own set of associations. A thirteen year old and a sixteen year old are separated out in our minds as likely to show certain characteristics. As far as motherhood is concerned there is an age when it is biologically possible to have a child, an age when marriage and therefore legitimate motherhood is legally possible and an age range when culturally it is seen as desirable to be a mother, and, indeed, deviant not to be. The age range when it is seen as desirable to become a mother varies but it very definitely excludes girls who are still at school.

The notion of maturity is significant both in terms of physical and psychological maturity but the culturally specific factors related to age have to be taken equally seriously. The school leaving age in a particular society will affect the impact of early motherhood on education, for example. The availability of educational resources, state benefits, housing, employment, child care, will also dictate the quality of life of the young mothers, their children, the fathers, and even their extended families in many cases. Thus it is clear at the outset, that the phenomenon of school age motherhood has to be seen as complex and socially structured.

The nature of motherhood, age and maturity appeared to be fundamental to the subject, but it was also obvious that an analysis of the experiences of young mothers had to consider issues of gender. Girls who are developing through adolescence into womanhood are by virtue of their pregnancies and their responsibilities as a mother, rapidly placed in a role seen traditionally as the heart of adult female identity. Are young mothers able to simultaneously become mothers and adults or does their early motherhood mark them out as deviant children?

The focus of this research became an exploration of how the young mother makes her way through pregnancy, birth and motherhood and how she comes to terms with her changing role. This involves what is both a methodological and theoretical dilemma: to what extent can outsider and insider perspectives as Phoenix (1991) puts it, be brought together in order to understand an event and the participant's experience of that event. As a piece of qualitative research, the emphasis here must be on exploring and valuing the insider perspectives of the young women. However, in order to look at the context, reference needs to be made to what is known from the literature about the circumstances in which school age mothers are thought to cope with pregnancy and motherhood.

Part I of this book, therefore, will consider the literature specifically relating to school age mothers and will also draw on other material that helps towards an understanding of the meaning of pregnancy and motherhood for young women. Although some of the literature draws on the views of young mothers, the balance is largely in favour of outsider perspectives on their backgrounds, motivations and needs.

Part II will contain an account of the methodology followed by a detailed analysis of interview material obtained from a number of young mothers. These were all women who had at some stage attended the tuition unit in Ipswich. The emphasis is on enabling the women to tell their own story and the only structure that is imposed on that process is the wish to consider the range of factors which affect their experience of the transition to motherhood. These factors may emerge from their personalities, their relationships, their circumstances or the services which they have been offered. The essence of this section is the meanings which young mothers attribute to their experiences.

In Part III the issues from the literature will be considered alongside the themes identified by the young mothers and the key elements of the outsider and the insider perspectives will be drawn together. It is hoped that not only will greater understanding of their experience be gained but that lessons may be learned about the kinds of resources that may enable school age mothers to incorporate motherhood successfully into their lives as young women.

Part I
SETTING THE SCENE: THEORY AND RESEARCH ON SCHOOL AGE PREGNANCY AND MOTHERHOOD

1 Background to the literature survey

The literature available specifically on school age mothers in Britain is very limited. It has emerged predominantly from concerns about the impact on a girl's education of early pregnancy and motherhood but there have also been concerns about the health and welfare of the mother and her child. On the whole, the literature has focused on the 'problem' of school age mothers and to this extent has been dominated by discussions about sexual activity and contraception with a view to prevention. In spite of the concern about the increasing rates of conception, the actual number of school age mothers is small which may be why large scale research projects, such as that set up by the Thomas Coram Research Foundation to explore the experiences of older teenage mothers (Phoenix 1991a), have not been attempted.

It is necessary to draw on a range of material about adolescent girls, sexuality and the ideologies of childhood and motherhood in order to find a way of understanding the experience of young mothers. Some material comes from American researchers, who have been more prolific in this area. There are a number of reasons for this. First, the 'problem' has an inherently wider definition in the United States because of the expectation that girls need to graduate from school at 18 in order to complete their education and have some chance of a career. Therefore, almost all teenage pregnancies are of concern. Secondly, comparisons made between the United States and certain European countries have found that although levels of sexual activity in the teenage years are similar, the rate of pregnancy in the United States is twice that of England and Wales and France, and six times that of the Netherlands. (Jones et al. 1986). Finally the sheer numbers of teenage mothers in the United States, i.e. over a million each year, represents a challenge to policy makers and planners and is also, as in this country, the subject of a great deal of media moralising and sensationalism.

Part I begins with an account of the statistical trends and then takes a chronological route through a young mother's experiences, starting with the impact of puberty, then addressing the issues of sexual activity, pregnancy, motherhood and the nature of services provided.

Relating as it does to trends in sexual behaviour and the changing nature of family life, the experience of school age mothers is likely to change in response to changes in the law, the benefits system, the education system and so on. These in turn will reflect and be reflected in public attitudes. Such trends will be identified where possible within the review of the literature.

The key questions to be answered appear to be:

1. What do we know about the factors involved when young women become pregnant while at school and decide to keep their babies?

2. Does the literature offer any explanation of how young women themselves make sense of their experiences?

This examination of the literature will thus provide a context for exploring the views of young mothers in Part II.

2   Statistics

The statistical trends regarding pregnancies occurring while girls are still of school age are not easy to establish. For the girls aged 15 or under the absolute figures and the rates can be obtained. For the 16 year olds it is not possible to be accurate about which pregnancies occurred while the girls were at school. Some will have left school at the time they become pregnant and others may have conceived while at school but leave school soon after, so that the pregnancy may not be known to school staff and there is no call on special educational or other resources.

Nevertheless, there are figures available for each year group and some general trends by age can be established. Bury (1984) has said that it is necessary to look at statistics over a ten year period in order to get an accurate picture of trends. However, the figures for school age pregnancies show interesting features when considered over a twenty year period and this will therefore be used here to identify trends.

Conceptions

If we consider the absolute numbers of conceptions, certain points emerge. The first is that there are fewer conceptions to both under sixteen year olds and sixteen year olds now than there were in the early seventies (see Figures 2.1 and 2.2). Secondly, although absolute numbers peaked again in the mid-eighties there has been a slight decline since then. These figures are affected by the numbers of girls in this age group in the population but nevertheless indicate that the demand by this age group for services has remained remarkably consistent over a long period of time.

Rates of conception show a different pattern (see Figures 2.3 and 2.4). Conception rates in 1989 were only slightly higher for under 16 year olds than in the early seventies (i.e. 9.5 per thousand compared to 9.3 in 1972).

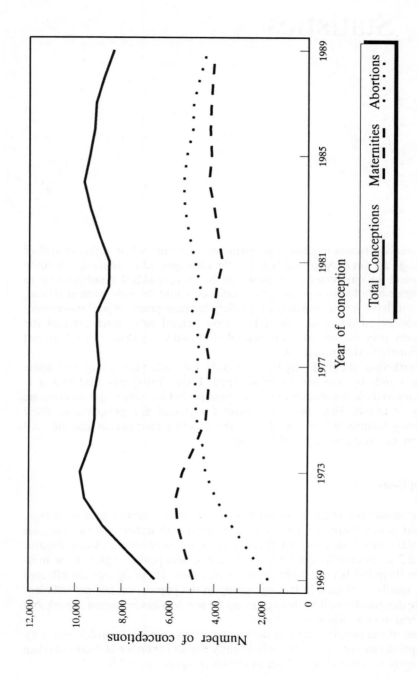

Figure 2.1: Teenage conceptions – under sixteen *(OPCS)*

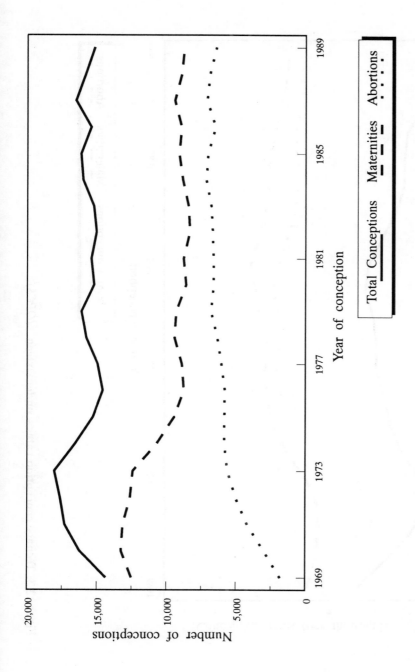

Figure 2.2: Teenage conceptions – age sixteen (*OPCS*)

7

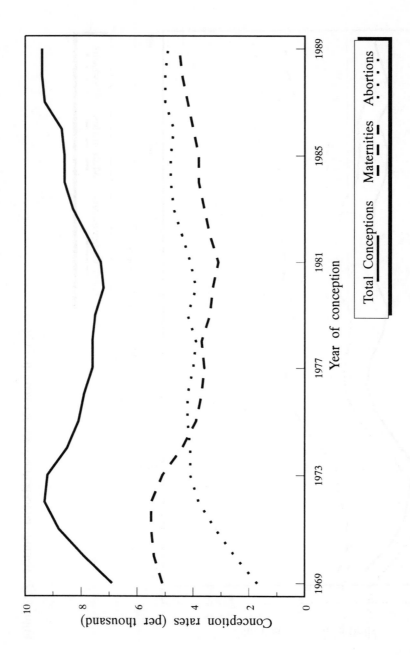

Figure 2.3: Teenage conception rates – under sixteen *(OPCS)*

Total Conceptions   Maternities   Abortions

8

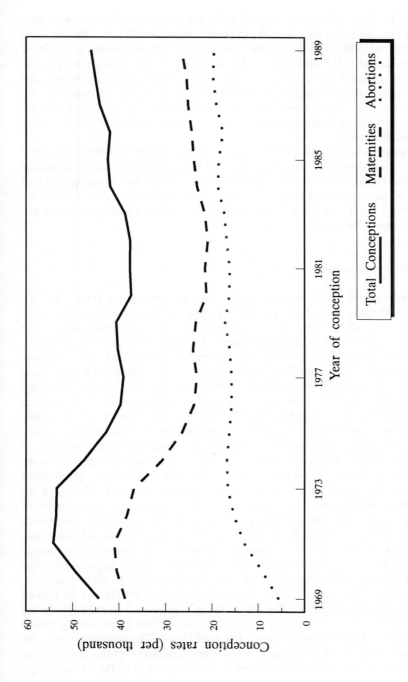

Figure 2.4: Teenage conception rates – age sixteen *(OPCS)*

Total Conceptions ——— Maternities – – – Abortions ·····

The rates for 16 year olds were significantly higher in the early seventies than in 1989 (i.e. 46.0 per thousand in 1989 compared to 54.1 per thousand in 1971). The trend through the eighties has been up in both groups, going from 7.2 per thousand to 9.5 for the under 16s and from 37.4 to 46.0 for the 16 year olds. Thus although the absolute numbers are not increasing at present, the upward trend in the rates since 1979 has been a source of concern. As mentioned earlier, the Government target is to reduce the rate for under 16 year olds by half, i.e. reducing the rate from the 1989 level of 9.5 per thousand to 4.8 per thousand.

This would take the rate well below that which existed in 1969 when only 2 per cent of girls aged 16 and under reported having had a sexual relationship (Schofield 1964). In 1990 the figure for sexual activity in this age group had risen to 48 per cent (Ford 1988). This factor will be considered in more detail in Chapter 2 but it needs to be born in mind at all times when these trends are identified and targets set.

Pregnancy outcomes

The proportion of those who choose to have the pregnancy terminated by abortion and those who proceed to delivery has changed over time and varies between age groups. The most significant changes occurred during the seventies. In 1969 the rates per thousand for under 16 year olds were 5.1 (maternities) and 1.7 (abortions). By the end of that decade the rates per thousand were 3.4 (maternities) and 4.2 (abortions). For the 16 year olds, maternities continued to outnumber abortions but the balance changed dramatically from 38.7 (maternities) and 5.6 (abortions) in 1969 to 23.5 (maternities) and 17.2 (abortions) in 1979. By 1989 the proportion was similar to that existing in 1979 for the sixteen year olds but the rates of maternities were moving closer to the rates for abortion in the under sixteen year olds.

Accurate figures for adoption as an outcome of school age pregnancy are impossible to obtain. This is not surprising since the secret nature of adoption has led to statistical records of adoptions being unavailable. Miles et al. (1979) suggested that around 12 per cent of school age pregnancies resulted in adoption. Birch (1987) gives a figure of 2 per cent in her group in Camberwell. Although as Howe, Sawbridge and Hinings (1992) have shown, adoption was once seen as the obvious choice for many illegitimate babies and in particular those born to young women, there appears to have been a major shift away from adoption as an outcome of choice for young women in recent years.

In summary, there have been no dramatic changes in the figures for school age motherhood since the availability of the pill decreased conceptions in the mid-seventies and the availability of abortion at around the same time increased the likelihood that pregnancies would be terminated. The increase in rates of conception among under sixteen year olds during the late eighties is the aspect of the figures which has caused concern to the Department of Health. Although improved family planning services and sex education are seen as necessary to reverse that trend this does not appear to have been based on any research into the reasons for the increase. There is need for more systematic research across the country if these figures are going to form the basis of government policy.

3   Adolescent girls and sexuality

> To write about children and sex is to bring together two sets of issues that are highly emotive, that readily provoke moral outrage and righteous indignation. (Jackson 1982 p. 1)

Before describing what the research literature has to say about girls who become pregnant while at school, it is necessary to consider the social and psychological context in which that pregnancy occurs. The reaction to the pregnancy by the girl herself, her family and society in general can only be understood if some attention is paid to the nature of adolescent sexuality and society's view of the appropriate moral boundaries which surround it. As Jackson points out above, childhood and sexuality are powerful elements in our consciousness and bringing them together is likely to produce strong reactions. The pregnant school girl threatens safe images of childhood and innocence.

In this chapter, the nature of adolescent development will be considered briefly together with the extent and context of sexual activity among young women still at school. The role of contraception will also be examined since this particular area of choice has to be exercised if sexually active young women are to have some control over their bodies and their lives.

Adolescence

Adolescence is traditionally seen as both the boundary between childhood and adulthood and also the process by which the transition from one to the other is achieved. Although the process is a gradual one, as Murcott (1980) says:

> It is the contrast not the continuity between childhood and adulthood which receives continual emphasis. (p. 7)

Most models of child development include some sequence of developmental stages (e.g. Piaget 1954, Erikson 1980). It is anticipated that certain tasks will be achieved at one level before moving on to the next. This sequential pattern does not readily accommodate the young mother who appears to be operating at an adult stage while still completing the tasks of a child. It is acceptable to be intellectually in advance of chronological age but other behaviours and roles are only acceptable at certain ages.

The physiological changes of puberty are the starting point of adolescence. As Rayner puts it:

> In its broadest sense, adolescence simply refers to psychological changes consequent upon puberty. (Rayner 1971, p. 104)

However, it is not possible to separate the impact of puberty from the ways in which adolescence is socially constructed. For the girl at the age of menarche, (which has dropped at a rate of 4 months every 10 years and is currently an average of 12 years 6 months), there are no other senses in which she has the identity of a woman. Incorporating the meaning of these bodily changes into her concept of self may be a difficult process. As Murcott (1980) puts it:

> Biologically a child becomes an adult earlier and earlier, socially a child becomes an adult later and later. (p. 8)

As the school leaving age has risen and there has been an expectation that larger numbers of young women will study or train beyond the school leaving age, the gap between the age at which girls mature and become capable of conceiving, and the age at which they might be reasonably expected to achieve economic independence, leave home, get married and become mothers, has increased. The difference between the age of menarche and the mean age of marriage is now 12 years. (Estaugh and Wheatley 1990)

The implication of being still defined as a child during the teenage years is that adults are expected to be in control. Murcott suggests that relations between children and adults are inherently between the powerless and powerful. Children are powerless, perhaps, but receive special treatment:

> Children are set apart from the rest of the population, regarded as a special category of people with their own needs. We have particular obligations towards them; we are expected to put their interest before our own. (Jackson 1982)

According to this line of thinking, children need to be educated about the world but also protected from it. Murcott and Jackson both take the view that current ideologies of childhood stress the essential innocence and dependence of children. So in the gap between physiological maturity and social maturity, girls in the early teenage years acquire information, ideas and values which should assist them while protecting them.

Within this broad framework, learning about sexuality carries on alongside physiological changes. Knowledge about reproduction is part of this but the range of information, ideas, and values about sexuality and relationships form a very complex package and come from a range of sources. Sex education at school is probably a minor source of information compared to television, family and friends. Nevertheless, schools have been criticised by most writers about school age pregnancy for failing to deal with the complex nature of relationships as part of sex education programmes. (Miles et al. (1979), Coyne (1986), Voydanoff and Donnelly (1990)). The Department of Education and Science advised schools to produce sex education programmes which include an examination of relationship issues in addition to the physiology of reproduction. (DES Circular No. 11/87 – Sex Education at School) The Government White Paper mentions that the Department of Education guidance emphasises schools' responsibility:

> to warn pupils of the health risks of casual and promiscuous sexual behaviour and to encourage pupils to have due regard to moral considerations, the value of family life and the responsibilities of parenthood. (Health of the Nation 1992)

Although such a debate may prove useful in improving the quality of sex education in school, girls make choices about their own sexual behaviour based on a wide range of ideas about themselves and the expectations of others. As Conger (1979) puts it:

> A major hurdle for both boys and girls at this stage is the successful integration of sexuality with other aspects of the emerging sense of self without having to undergo too much conflict and anxiety. (p. 52)

Sexual activity

Rates

The changing patterns of sexual activity over the last twenty years has not been well documented. Most literature has been based on two research projects, one by Schofield (1964) and one by Farrell (1978). Their research looked at both the patterns of sexual activity in different age groups and the attitudes of young people towards sexual relationships. Although their work was detailed and helpful, research based on attitudes in the mid-seventies does have limited value in explaining attitudes in the early nineties. Recent research by Ford (1988) goes some way to bringing this information up to date but his survey was of urban and rural areas in the southwest of England and clearly a more varied pattern might be found if major cities and areas of greater cultural and ethnic diversity in other parts of the country were included.

However, with this proviso, Ford's figures do suggest a dramatic increase in the level of sexual activity in recent years

Table 3.1
Young people claiming an experience of sexual intercourse before 16 years of age

	Boys	Girls
Schofield (1964)	6%	2%
Farrell (1978)	26%	12%
Ford (1988)	36%	48%

Source: Estaugh and Wheatley, 1990

When nearly half of sixteen year old girls report having experienced intercourse, this group clearly cannot be seen as a deviant minority. The dramatic increase in the last ten years suggests a major change in behaviour and inevitably begs the question as to whether this indicates a change in attitude by young people themselves to the idea that engaging in sexual relationships while of school age has become more acceptable, morally and socially.

The second key finding by Ford (1988) is that there are now more sexually active girls than boys at the age of 16. This finding does not appear to have been explained and could indicate a range of possible changes in behaviour and attitudes. The most simple explanation may be that girls are more likely to have relationships with older boys. Possibly a few boys have relationships with a larger number of girls. This, however, cannot be clarified without a great deal more detailed research than we have at present.

The age of consent

These figures need also to be looked at in a range of different contexts. The most obvious and striking factor is that by having intercourse before the age of 16 years, a very large number of girls are involved in an activity that defines them as victims of a crime. The age of consent arose originally from the Criminal Law Amendment Act (1885). The age of menarche at that time would have been around 16. According to Miles et al. (1979), this piece of legislation was designed to prevent young girls from being drawn into prostitution. It takes for granted that the girls would not be able to give consent and would be exploited therefore in any sexual relationship. The criminal offence is that of unlawful sexual intercourse not rape so the model of behaviour it is based on seems likely to be more like that of persuasion or seduction, i.e. the girl is persuaded to have intercourse against her better judgement. If there were an element of force, the offence would be different.

The implications of this legislation for girls are far-reaching. It suggests that the state has deemed that sexual intercourse for those under the age of sixteen is so evidently wrong, that no girl could reasonably give consent to it. Girls are not seen as able to make choices about their sexuality but as needing the protection of the state. The legislation does not discriminate between teenagers who are being abused or exploited sexually and those who may be in sexual relationships by choice.

The Joint Working Party (1979) concluded that having an age of consent of 16 was counterproductive because it criminalized an activity about which a degree of openness was necessary. If girls were to be able to discuss their sexual relationships, and in particular seek contraceptive advice, then an atmosphere of fear in terms of the consequences for their partners was not helpful and merely compounded the problems. It is particularly significant that this conclusion was reached by a multi-agency group who were considering the situation at a time when only twelve per cent of this age group were reporting sexual activity. Even in that context they reached what was for them a difficult conclusion. Given the four hundred per cent increase in levels of sexual activity since 1979, it is surprising that the issue is not being debated more energetically. In fact, in 1991, when the Dutch government legalised heterosexual and homosexual intercourse above the age of 12, there was an outcry in the British media. Britain seems reluctant to consider whether a law which is rarely enforced but which criminalizes and creates anxiety in an already emotionally complex area may be disadvantaging rather than protecting girls under the age of 16. In a society which now deals with the complex issue of consent when considering the offence of rape within marriage or on a date, it should be possible to determine the nature of consent for those under the age of sixteen. This is a difficult issue but needs raising as part of the context of sexual behaviour in adolescence.

Peer group culture

There has been a certain amount of research into the nature of peer group relationships and the climate of attitudes and values which affect sexual choices. Bury (1984) concluded that although more teenagers are having sexual intercourse at a younger age, there is no evidence that teenagers are more likely to have casual sexual relationships. Farrell (1978) found that 80 per cent of those in sexual relationships had been 'going out' with their partner for more than six months. There seemed to be some evidence of what Bury refers to as 'serial monogamy' in which sexual behaviour is still 'regulated by such traditional values as love, fidelity, partnership, marriage and the family.' (Bury 1984 p. 34)

More recent research has looked at the issue from a rather different perspective. Lees (1986) has been particularly influential in developing ideas around the social construction of sexuality. By focusing attention on the use of insults and the significance of sexual reputation, she identifies the problems for girls in making choices about their sexual behaviour:

> The commonest insult, used by both sexes, is 'slag'. But all the insults in frequent use seem to relate to a girl's sexual reputation. It is crucial to note that the insults might bear no relation at all to a girl's actual sexual behaviour. But this does not make things any easier for the girls. An unjustified tag can stick as easily as a justified one. (Lees 1986 p. 37)

What emerges from Lees' research is that sexual insults label not just the sexual behaviour but the whole person. Similarly any aspect of behaviour – choice of clothes, tone of voice, attitude, can earn the label of 'slag'. Because of the power of the label and the comprehensive way in which it was applied, it was impossible to argue against it.

Lees found that there was no equivalent label which girls could use about boys and the range of behaviour that was acceptable in boys was often unchallenged by girls:

> What is of particular interest here is the operation of an ideology that transforms the experience of very unfair relations between the sexes into an acceptance of those relations as natural. It is somehow wrong and horrible for a girl to invite sexual activity but somehow natural for the boy to be after it, to attempt to pester you into it, to tell if you do and to fabricate its occurrence if you don't. If a girl contravenes this code, she deserves to be beaten up. (Lees 1986 p. 49)

What is most difficult for girls, it seems, is that the label is also likely to be applied by one girl to another. The level of anxiety that is created is such that far from being united against the imposition of labels by boys, girls wish to disassociate themselves from any girl who might appear to have earned the label and would then apply the label themselves. This restricts, according to Lees, the freedom of girls who can become very reluctant to engage in a social life let alone make choices about a sexual relationship because of the pressures and the difficulties.

The only way out of this dilemma, it seems, is to have a steady boyfriend: this legitimates a sexual relationship:

> Few girls were clear about what being in love means though invariably love is given as the only legitimate reason for sleeping with a boy. The importance of love seems to be, therefore, in its permitting feelings of sexual excitement while offering some protection from a reputation of sluttishness. (Lees 1986 p. 51)

Given that context, it seems that girls may continue in unsatisfactory relationships because of the fear of breaking the 'in love' code of acceptable sex. This may be the other side of the situation described by Bury (see above).

Perhaps it is not only the traditional values of 'love, fidelity' etc. which regulate sexual behaviour but fear of the loss of sexual reputation.

This research, undertaken by Lees in the early 80s, was clearly picking up themes, some of which go back to traditional values such as that of the double standard and the link between love relationships and sexual relationships. New theories have to accommodate changing attitudes such as that sex outside marriage is not in itself viewed critically. It seems likely that in the ten years since that research, attitudes are now having also to accommodate the fact that nearly fifty per cent of girls are sexually active by the age of sixteen. Bowie and Ford (1989), for example, found among older teenagers that 15–24 per cent believe that sexual intercourse is acceptable outside a steady relationship – a category they call 'casual-recreational'. It is not possible yet to know whether this attitude has spread to the younger age group and their figures do not distinguish between girls and boys. They also take no account of Lees' theory about the relevance of reputation. The impact of AIDS education programmes on decisions about sexual relationships has also yet to be tested.

In addition to the research into attitudes, there has been some research into the likely backgrounds of those who become sexually active at an early age. In the United States, Voydanoff and Donnelly conclude their review thus:

> The young people with the fewest resources, those who are poorer, less educated, non-white, from the least stable families and who have the poorest life chances are the ones who are most apt to become sexually active when they are quite young. (Voydanoff and Donnelly 1990 p. 41)

What is not obvious is the nature of the causal relationship between poor life chances and sexual activity at an early age. More needs to be known about the meaning that girls attach to their sexual activity. Is it that young girls with 'poor life chances' feel less bound by conventional morality or is it that early sexual activity has become conventional morality for certain groups in society? Without having a clear and up to date picture of the norms and values within particular groups of young people, it is not clear whether sexual relationships are a source of self-esteem and contribute to a positive sense of identity or whether they are stigmatised and contribute to a loss of self-esteem for girls. It seems likely that issues of power and choice are important in considering whether girls who have poor life chances and have few areas of choice, make a choice about their sexual relationships. Whatever the context, it is certain that as Lees (1986) has pointed out, those choices are made from socially constructed alternatives.

In spite of the private nature of sexual behaviour, it has always been subject to social controls and certainly the sexual behaviour of young people cannot be separated from the mores of the society in which they live. The research dilemma is how to describe such a complex and constantly changing phenomenon. As Voydanoff and Donnelly conclude:

18

A number of social, economic, family, peer, and biological factors help to predict which young people will initiate sexual activity at early ages. These factors are, of course, closely interlinked, each is related in complex ways to the others. (Voydanoff and Donnelly (1990) p. 41)

Thus defining the web of factors which may have affected any specific young woman is likely to prove impossible.

Contraception

In view of all the factors that contribute to the complexity of young women's decisions about sexual relationships, it is not surprising that it has been difficult to analyse the pattern of decision making in the area of contraceptive use. In this section, three key areas will be addressed: knowledge, availability and use of contraception.

Knowledge

There seems to be an almost unanimous view that good information about contraception as part of sex education within schools is an essential starting point.

Appropriate teaching about responsible sexual behaviour should start in the first years of the secondary school curriculum and should include specific and accurate information about contraception. (Miles et al. 1979)

More recent researchers have criticised both the timing and the content of sex education in general (Hudson and Ineichen 1991, Coyne 1986) and it appears that information about contraception and in particular the problems for young people in making choices and using contraception are not dealt with fully enough or early enough in school. Although there are DES circulars on the provision of sex education, responsibility for its provision has been left to a process of negotiation between each school and its Board of Governors, so variations are likely to continue.

Attitudes to such education in schools are often only reflections of society's uncertainty. A report from the Royal College of Obstetricians and Gynaecologists suggested that:

Britain must overcome its confused, complex and contradictory attitude to sex if use of contraception is to increase and the growing number of abortions is to be checked. (Reported in *The Guardian* 4th September 1991.)

The report emphasised the role of sex education but it is difficult to know how a society's attitude to sex can be changed in order for that education itself to be as comprehensive as the college recommends. Surely sex education for the foreseeable future is likely to reflect the 'confused' and 'contradictory' attitudes in society as a whole.

Availability

The debate over the Gillick case placed the issue of contraception in the forefront of an important debate about the rights of young people, in particular young women, to make decisions about their lives and their bodies. The ruling of the House of Lords (1985) was that Mrs Victoria Gillick could not prevent her daughters from being prescribed the contraceptive pill by withholding her consent. However, although the ruling is often quoted as giving rights to girls under the age of sixteen, the right to contraception now depends on the judgement of the doctor rather than the judgement of the parent.

> The Gillick decision stated that a medical practitioner, providing contraceptive advice for a girl under 16 without informing parents was not in breach of the law if he believed:
>
> (i) that the girl (although under 16 years of age) will understand his advice;
>
> (ii) that he cannot persuade her to inform her parents or to allow him to inform the parents that she is seeking contraceptive advice;
>
> (iii) that she is very likely to begin or to continue to have sexual intercourse with or without contraceptive treatment;
>
> (iv) that unless she receives contraceptive advice or treatment, her physical or mental health or both are likely to suffer;
>
> (v) that her best interests require him to give her contraceptive advice, treatment or both without the parental consent.' (Lord Fraser, House of Lords, quoted in Kendell and Coleman 1988)

The girl has to convince the doctor of a number of quite difficult matters and the doctor then relies on his own judgement and presumably his own values as to what he deems to be in her best interests. The use of the male pronoun for the doctor reminds us of a further difficulty. A young girl may have to discuss her sexual choices with a man, likely to be equivalent to her father or grandfather in age.

A key element to emerge in the debate of the Gillick case was that the maturity of the individual must be considered to be more relevant than a specific chronological age. At the first stage of the case, Mr Justice Woolf in the High Court ruled:

> Whether or not a child is capable of giving the necessary consent (to medical treatment) will depend upon the child's maturity and understanding and the nature of the consent which is required.

The Court of Appeal supported Mrs Gillick's view that she should decide what was in her children's best interests:

> Parents have 'a right and duty to determine the place and manner in which a child's time is spent' and this includes the right and duty to control the child subject to the intervention of the Court. There must be a fixed age in order that parents, children and those dealing with children may know where they stand and what are their powers, rights and duties or obligations. (Lord Justice Parker in Gillick – Court of Appeal 1984)

The House of Lords reversed the ruling of the Court of Appeal. Lord Fraser criticised the idea that maturity is achieved at a certain age or that parental control should continue longer than necessary:

> In practice most wise parents relax their control gradually as the child develops and encourage him or her to become increasingly independent. Moreover, the degree of parental control actually exercised over a particular child does in practice vary considerably according to his understanding and intelligence and it would be unrealistic for the Courts not to recognise those facts. (Lord Fraser in Gillick – House of Lords 1985)

However, even in the House of Lords judgement there was a dissenting voice which suggested, by implication, the popular view that removing the possibility of contraception makes sex among young girls less likely:

> I doubt whether a girl under the age of 16 is capable of a balanced judgement to embark on frequent, regular or casual sexual intercourse, fortified by the illusion that medical science can protect her in mind and body and ignoring the danger of leaping from childhood to adulthood without the difficult formative transitional experiences of adolescence. There are many things that a girl under 16 needs to practise but sex is not one of them. (Lord Templeman in Gillick, minority view House of Lords 1985)

These views are quoted at length because they encapsulate a much broader debate about the nature of maturity and the transition from childhood to adulthood which occurs during the adolescent years. What is more the Gillick decision emphasises the need for young people to be treated as individuals. Whether or not a person has the ability to form a judgment on a particular issue can only be assessed by knowledge of a particular young person, not on the basis of generalisations based on chronological age.

As far as the giving of contraceptive advice was concerned, the judgements were still equivocal about the rights and wrongs of under sixteen year olds having sexual intercourse – not surprisingly given the law on the age of consent. The emphasis was on contraceptives as a medical treatment and it was compared in the judgement to seeking treatment for a broken arm. It was on that basis that doctors were freed of the fear that they might be guilty of the criminal offence of aiding and abetting the commission of unlawful sexual intercourse by providing contraceptives.

Although the Gillick ruling was clear about the confidentiality and right to treatment of a girl who was deemed to be both at risk and of mature judgement, it did not ensure confidentiality where the girl was not deemed by the doctor to be of mature judgement. In 1986 the General Medical Council ruled that General Practitioners were allowed to break confidentiality in those circumstances. This issue is still being debated but at present the availability of confidential consultations about contraception cannot be guaranteed to a young woman under the age of sixteen.

Use

Knowledge about contraception and the availability of contraceptives is only the starting point. Researchers have struggled to deal with the much more difficult issue of the motivation and ability of young people to use contraception effectively. Some researchers have concluded that knowledge of contraception is only marginally related to contraceptive use. (McGrew and Shore 1991)

Birch (1987) and Lees (1986) concluded that girls were more anxious that they should not be seen as 'cheap' or 'easy' than they were to be sure to prevent unwanted pregnancies. Any form of contraception requires planning and involves an admission that the possibility of sexual intercourse had been anticipated.

Although these writers emphasise the anxiety which girls experience at the label which boys may apply to them – the fear of being defined as a 'slag'– it seems likely that girls themselves are unsure of their own feelings regarding sex and may not themselves want to commit themselves consciously to the idea of a sexual relationship.

Although these arguments go some way to explaining why many young couples do not use contraception the first time they have intercourse (Farrell 1978), and the majority of girls attending Family Planning clinics have already had unprotected sex, they do not explain why even within a steady relationship the use of contraception is not consistent. Ineichen (1986) suggests that ambivalence about the possibility of pregnancy is part of the picture but there is no clear-cut evidence as to the extent of this as a factor.

Perhaps research into the use of the condom and the spread of Aids may give us some clues about the nature of decision making.

> It is trite to think that safe sex adoption is simply a question of will for many women. Sex is often a much more complex behaviour, affected by the extent to which woman are empowered to negotiate their sex and the costs to them of withholding such sex. (Mihill 1992)

The role of power and the need for women to be empowered in the arena of sexual behaviour is a matter which must be addressed if some of the apparent contradictions are to be understood and resolved.

4 Pregnancy

From what is known about contraceptive use among girls of school age for whom contraception is not even easily available, it seems doubtful that the decision not to use contraception or the practice of not using contraception effectively can be seen as indicative of a wish to become pregnant. The wish to become pregnant plays a relatively small part in distinguishing the group of sexually active girls who become pregnant from those who don't. Miles et al. (1979) concluded:

> Most pregnant schoolgirls differ from their non-pregnant peers only by reason of their pregnancy. (p. 11)

Coyne (1986) suggests that for the most part pregnant schoolgirls may be just the unlucky ones. This, however, needs to be looked at in more detail since it affects assumptions that become part of society's attitude to these girls and may affect how the girls themselves view their pregnancies.

There is some confusion in the literature between analysis of the possible reasons for becoming pregnant and the possible motivations for deciding to keep the baby once the pregnancy is confirmed. Such confusion frequently links becoming pregnant and deciding to keep the baby as characterised by similar psychological factors. For example:

> Girls, those who become pregnant and typically those who keep their baby, tend to find difficulty in making and sustaining good relationships and yet a good relationship is what they most need. (Hudson & Ineichen 1991 p. 108)

It seems, however, important to distinguish between becoming pregnant and the decision to keep the baby since they may indicate quite different issues for each girl.

Becoming pregnant

There have been a number of attempts to describe the group of girls who become pregnant at school in terms of their backgrounds. Most commonly mentioned is the greater likelihood that those who become pregnant come from lower socio-economic groups. (Russell, 1982, Simms and Smith 1986, Coyne 1986, Birch 1986). The explanation for such a link is varied. Russell comments:

> ... the young group come from families where there is less discipline, and less control over their behaviour. I find that young girls from the upper socio-economic classes are more likely to be chaperoned and watched more carefully at the ages of 14, 15, and 16. (Russell, 1982, p. 72)

Russell views early pregnancy as a form of deviance which he links to other 'social problems' such as having parents who are separated, divorced, or in jail. He also sees it as a symptom of excessive sexual activity and lack of self-discipline and restraint. Although his value-laden text appears to reflect a minority view, Dr. Russell is a Professor of Obstetrics and Gynaecology and is much quoted. In fact, a recent publication on teenage motherhood criticises the fact that Russell's work is not mentioned by more researchers. (Hudson and Ineichen, 1991)

A link is also made between social deprivation, psychological problems and pregnancy:

> A less esoteric formulation is that early pregnancy is the end link in a chain of events starting with social or family deprivation and leading through boredom, feelings of rejection or depression to gratification of personal needs by heterosexual activity and childbirth. (Schaffer et al. 1978)

This supports the idea of a chain of events but does not spell out in what ways the relationship between events is causal. Does social deprivation lead to feelings of rejection? Is it the heterosexual activity or the childbirth or both which gratify personal needs? The authors themselves seem unsure of their ground and offer an alternative:

> An alternative explanation requires no psycho-pathological premise. This would propose that pregnancy is an inadvertent consequence of a normal erotic relationship in itself desired and rewarding, abnormal only in that the usual social taboos had not been effective and that one or both partners have had inadequate access to knowledge about or motivation to use efficient methods of birth control. (Shaffer et al. 1978 p. 120)

The large numbers of sexually active young people, the vague nature of the 'usual social taboos' and the lack of appropriate contraceptive services for young people suggests that the 'abnormal' element is uncertain. It is interesting that the reference to 'a normal erotic relationship' is not common in the recent literature on school age pregnancy although researchers thirty years ago

24

reached a similar conclusion. Anderson et al. (1960) found that the majority of adolescent pregnancies:

> ... followed on naturally enough from the pursuit of adolescent practices normal to the whole society ... The context was one of a normal erotic relationship, sometimes but not always comprehended by the girl as a personal love relationship. (Anderson et al. 1960. p. 357)

Some other recent writers also reject the conclusion that the link between socio-economic class and early pregnancy is via psychopathology. Birch (1986) suggests that the issue of school age pregnancy is predominantly related to lack of opportunities in education and careers for girls from lower socio-economic groups and is inclined to see early pregnancy as in many ways a logical way of finding a role in life. Her view is supported by Ineichen (1986):

> Many of the teenagers may have felt that there was no good reason for delaying pregnancy. Motherhood is highly valued throughout society and an invariable route to full adult status. Given the unemployment rate prevailing among working class teenagers it becomes meaningful to ask not why so many pregnant teenagers but why so few? (Ineichen 1986 p. 392)

Finally this view is reflected in the Family Policy Studies Centre document, which having stressed at length the high rate of sexual activity among young people, concludes its chapter on teenage pregnancy thus:

> They may see motherhood as the only worthwhile creative thing they can do. (Estaugh and Wheatley 1990 p. 46)

There are two main problems with this line of argument when it is applied specifically to school age pregnancies. First, it seems less likely that the younger teenage group would see pregnancy as a reasonable alternative to school or future employment in the way older teenagers are said to see it as alternative to current unemployment. Secondly, all arguments about motivation to become pregnant assume that the pregnancy was a choice, that the sexual relationship and lack of contraception was deliberately aimed at achieving pregnancy. This is not supported by the literature. It is important to distinguish between those who, as Birch describes, live in areas of massive social deprivation and lack the motivation or means to prevent pregnancy and those who are said to choose pregnancy as an alternative to unemployment. Birch, herself, found that only 2 per cent of pregnant schoolgirls considered their pregnancy to be planned.

It has sometimes been suggested that the wish to be pregnant is an unconscious rather than a conscious wish, what Hudson and Ineichen (1991) refer to as 'More direct motives for pregnancy, but still possibly beneath the girls' level of awareness.' This is followed by a list which goes further than that of Shaffer et al. (1978) (see above):

Where life at home may be unhappy for the girl for a variety of reasons; where she has not experienced warmth and affection to satisfy her needs; where parents have shown inconsistency and ambivalence in their relating patterns generally; where the parents are separated, divorced, arguing and/or fighting; where a single mother is too involved in the emotional and physical struggle with her own relationship to cope with her children – any one of these sets of circumstances could motivate pregnancy in the teenage daughter. (Hudson and Ineichen 1991 p. 40)

Although features from this list undoubtedly occur in the life histories of some girls who become pregnant while at school, there are few studies which look statistically at the links between such characteristics and pregnancy in a way that suggests they provide a motivation for pregnancy. Grouping early pregnancy in this way with a range of what are seen as social problems reflects a blanket prejudice against all family configurations that vary from an idealised nuclear family. Moreover, early pregnancy is experienced by only a small minority of young women who have been exposed to the circumstances listed by Hudson and Ineichen; the factors identified can hardly be causal, therefore.

Wilson (1980) conducted a study of girls in Aberdeen who became pregnant before the age of 16. Wilson's study group was derived from the Aberdeen Child Development Study (ACDS) from which a large amount of information was available. The children had all been born between October 1950 and September 1955. Forty-four girls from this group who became pregnant when they were under the age of 16 were studied. Wilson concluded that compared to a group matched on socio-demographic characteristics pregnant girls were more likely to have been academic underachievers at 11, to have made an appearance in a juvenile court, and to have been referred to a child guidance or psychiatric clinic. Because of difficulties over matching, Wilson suggests they may also be more likely to have five or more siblings, to be illegitimate and to have mothers who were themselves teenagers at the time of their daughter's birth. Wilson drew up a table of risk scores using these risk factors.

Table 4.1: Adolescent pregnancy risk scores

Risk Factors	Girls known to have become pregnant before 16 years		Rest of Population	
	No.	%	No.	%
0	9	34.6	2543	59.6
1	10	38.5	1383	32.4
2	3	11.5	294	6.9
3+	4	15.4	45	1.1
Total	26	100.0	4265	100.0

Source: Wilson, 1980

These figures are important in indicating that there are a number of different risk factors but they still need to be treated with caution. As can be seen from the above table, 34.6 per cent of the index group had none of the risk factors identified and 38.5 per cent had only one risk factor. What is even more important is that although pregnant girls under the age of 16 may be *more likely* than their peer group to have certain characteristics, this is often misread to mean that the *majority* of these girls have these characteristics. Inaccurate quoting of research can also give this impression. Hudson and Ineichen (1991) refer to American research and add:

> Like Wilson's sample, most were themselves children of young mothers. (p. 107)

The correct reading of Wilson's figures is that the vast majority of girls (i.e. 89 per cent) who become pregnant before the age of 16 were not born to mothers under the age of 20. Hudson and Ineichen also refer to Coyne's research group saying 'several of whom, like Wilson's had been in trouble with the law.' (Hudson and Ineichen 1991 p. 107) In fact, Coyne chose to interview residents at a community home for pregnant girls and mothers, who were juvenile offenders, as part of her research, so the implication that Coyne has shown an association between delinquency and early pregnancy is not accurate.

There is a need to be clear about the detail of the small amount of research that is available because otherwise it can only too readily contribute to stereotyping young pregnant girls. The assumption that a pregnant girl is merely following in her mother's footsteps adds a sense of inevitability and fatalism which can be counterproductive and denies the individuality of the girl and the complexity of the situation. The case of the thirteen year old girl whose mother was 26 and whose grandmother was 46 is mentioned by Birch (1987) and quoted again by Hudson and Ineichen (1991). Such examples make sensational reading but should not be allowed to dominate our view of the situation for young mothers in the absence of more comprehensive research over a range of communities. As Melhuish and Phoenix (1987) point out:

> In view of the problems of comparing teenage mothers and their children with other groups, it would be more productive to use the variability within the group of mothers under 20 to gain a better understanding of the range and operation of potent factors in their lives. (p. 294)

This seems to be equally true of mothers who become pregnant while at school.

Making the decision

In order for young girls to make a decision about the outcome of pregnancy they need to have the opportunity to weigh up information about the different

27

outcomes and then consider their own feelings, ideas and values. This process is not well documented and appears to be the subject of much speculation:

> Even though conception may have been accidental, the girls had sufficient emotional deficits to produce intensive need for fulfilment, meaning, status, importance, love – all of which could be envisaged as coming about through a child. (Zongker 1977 p. 487)

This tendency to suggest that the decision to keep the child is confirmation that the young mother is psychologically damaged is common. (See also Coyne 1986)

Sometimes it is suggested that it is the young woman's family background that leads to this decision (Landy et al. 1983). Landy describes such a household as 'Mother ridden', a particularly unpleasant expression, with the father being the weaker partner.

To suggest that pregnant young women who decide to keep their babies are psychologically unsound or do not understand the difficulties they will face has led to some implicit assumptions that abortion or relinquishing the child for adoption are the 'right' courses of action. Few writers have felt inclined to make this explicit but Hudson and Ineichen (1991) appear to be fairly unequivocal:

> Pregnant schoolgirls who decide themselves on a termination or who do not keep the baby once born – these girls are most likely to appreciate their schooling and to want to realise their potential in terms of education and career (see particularly McGuire 1983) and to have full parental support in this view. In such cases the girls have families who are truly supportive and are not so needy themselves as to deprive their daughter of her own vision of her future. Sensible and sensitive decisions can be made, bearing in mind all that is at stake and putting the adolescent and her need first. (Hudson and Ineichen 1991 p. 109)

There seems to be quite a circular argument here which needs to be clarified. There is some evidence from the United States (Voydanoff and Donnelly 1991) that girls who choose termination are more likely to have a better academic record and be ambitious. However, Hudson and Ineichen link this idea with the suggestion that 'truly supportive' parents, who are not emotionally needy, would not offer support to their daughter in keeping the child. Should we tend therefore to suspect that girls who decide to keep their babies lack ambition or that parents who support them should be suspected of meeting their own emotional needs? This seems to be a dangerous argument and is extended to include the idea that parents may be 'conspiratorial':

> Inevitably the younger the girl the less experience she has of decision-making, the less knowledge she has and the more she has experienced external (family) control. As has already been discussed, a girl in her early teens will tend initially to deny the pregnancy and subsequently to

absolve herself from all responsibility. Contradictory as it may seem, if both these factors are accompanied by conspiratorial parents (whether consciously or unconsciously) the girl is very likely to insist on becoming a mother. (Hudson and Ineichen p. 111)

The mother's decision to keep the baby is seen as arising from a number of possible causes – they quote eighteen – all of which are negative and revolve around fear, pressure, suspicion, disaffection from parents and school etc. The one possibly positive reason is seen as pathological:

> To have an object to love. To have something to call your own. For those who have never had anything or are forever losing what they have got. To satisfy a need for a loving and dependent relationship. To have someone who demands constant attention and affection. (Hudson and Ineichen 1991 p. 43)

Hudson and Ineichen (1991) look at the decisions open to the pregnant girl and conclude that since the motives for keeping the child are all flawed and since abortion is said to be undesirable for a young teenager, the choice of adoption is left. Although they acknowledge that this is currently the least acceptable option to teenagers, they suggest that for a clear thinking girl with proper counselling, relinquishing the child should be the desired outcome. Referring to several girls who gave up their children for adoption they conclude:

> No one will deny that giving up the baby is hard. It represents loss in the true sense and requires an unspecified period of mourning – but it is the positive, indeed the realistic vision of the future together with continuous support both from professionals and from the family that allow the mother to take this generous course of action. (p. 96)

This is contrasted with girls who keep their babies.

> Thus it is that the young woman who is least able to sort through the pressures and confusion, more often than not ends up by keeping the baby and convincing herself that on all counts she has done the morally right thing. (p. 96)

Many of these statements by Hudson and Ineichen (1991) reflect views that prevailed in the 1950s and indeed were being challenged even then. This quotation comes from a Public Affairs Pamphlet published in 1959:

> Unfortunately, many of the girls who keep their babies are those who seem least able to do it well. These are the girls who are deprived emotionally themselves and cling to the baby as their one possession feeling that it will make up to them for other lacks in their lives. (Butcher and Robinson 1959)

Whatever the choice of outcome, Birch (1987) suggests, it is important that girls are enabled to make the choice themselves without undue pressure. However, the choice of keeping the baby appears to attract a whole range of negative images, both about the mother and, significantly, her parents. It is perhaps not surprising that society in general is inclined to see young mothers as a symptom of moral decline and social ill.

5 Motherhood

Images of motherhood

In order to put young mothers in their social and psychological context it is important to consider the prevailing images of motherhood in our society. This is because of the role that motherhood plays in the imagination and sense of identity of young mothers and also the role these images play in determining how families, schools, or even people at the bus-stop react to the idea of a fifteen year old mother. Although some aspects of motherhood may be seen in a similar light by the young women and those around them, the actual experience of early motherhood may well give young women a viewpoint that is not shared by others. When it comes to motherhood which occurs outside what is seen as the acceptable age range, there is potential for conflict.

Most writers on school age pregnancy or, more broadly, teenage pregnancy, mention the fact that girls are socialised into believing that motherhood is their destiny and is to be a major source of fulfilment as women. (Cunningham 1984, Lees 1986, Spender and Sarah 1980, Neustatter 1986) To this extent it would seem that school girls who become mothers are simply achieving that part of their destiny at too early an age. However, as with early sexual activity, early motherhood is generally seen not as a sign of early adulthood but as a sign of deviant childhood.

The link between motherhood and maturity is a fundamental issue:

> Motherhood also bestows positive identity on women. Motherhood is highly valued symbolically as the key to adulthood; having a child makes a woman a mother *and* an adult. (Woollett 1991 (emphasis in original) p. 53)

So having children is associated with being an adult but is becoming a mother evidence of having previously become a mature adult or is the process of becoming a mother in itself a maturing process? Woollett continues:

31

Women who do not have children may experience difficulties in being recognised as fully adult and grown up people. (p. 53)

This argument suggests that adult status for women is not so easily achieved by other means, for example simply by growing older, taking on work responsibilities and so on. It adds weight to the idea that becoming a mother in itself contributes to the achievement of adulthood.

Although having a baby can be seen as making a mother out of a woman it also confirms her identity as a woman:

Motherhood is symbolically important too because it confirms women's female identity and is in this respect central to their sense of themselves. It demonstrates women's physical and psychological adequacy and, as producers of the next generation, gives them identifiable social functions. (Woollett 1991 p. 57)

Thus motherhood has a very comprehensive impact on a woman by confirming her adult female identity, asserting her competence and giving her a role. However, the positive image of motherhood that prevails has been repeatedly questioned by researchers who find that in fact depression and loss of self-esteem are frequently associated with motherhood, (Brown and Harris 1978, Oakley 1979, Richman 1978). Oakley concluded that it was the gap between idealised expectations of motherhood and the reality of day to day mothering which caused stress.

The experience of motherhood

Boulton (1983) took a more detailed look at the different features of the experience of being a mother. She distinguished between a mother's feeling of enjoyment or irritation with the work involved in caring for children and the extent to which women experienced a sense of meaning and purpose in their role as mother. Half of the women in her study found child care 'a predominantly frustrating and irritating experience' but two-thirds experienced a sense of meaning and purpose in their role as mothers. (p. 205)

Significantly, she found that working class women were less likely to experience a conflict between how they saw child care and the meaning of motherhood. They were on the whole more likely to say they enjoyed the task of caring for children. Perhaps the gap identified by Oakley between expectations and reality arose from the fact that her sample was from professional middle class women. Depression among working class mothers may be linked to a different combination of factors.

For young mothers, and in particular those who give birth while of school age, it is not anticipated from the outset that motherhood will be associated for them with the confirmation of identity and the provision of a clear role to play. Phoenix and Woollett (1991) propose that there is an 'implicit, socially ideal age span' and that young mothers are 'contradictorily positioned because they are devalued when they enter a status that is supposedly women's supreme achievement.' (p. 9)

Coyne (1986) interviewed thirty school age mothers and gives detailed case histories based on interviews in her report for the Health Education Council. Out of the twenty-seven young women who had given birth prior to the interview, twenty-six described a range of on balance positive aspects of their experience of becoming a mother. Although some of these respondents talked of the role as being harder work than they had anticipated, they all identified the experience as having positive elements. One theme that seemed important was the feeling of being more mature and having a purpose in life. This was associated not only with the role of caring for the baby but also with working harder for examinations, and thinking seriously about pursuing a career.

Linked with this feeling of greater maturity was the fact that the young mother's parents treated her as more mature and adult and although there were variations in the family responses to the pregnancy, the majority felt supported by their families after the birth. Thus referring back to Boulton's categories (p. 39) it would seem that the young women in Coyne's study had gained some sense of meaning and purpose from their role as mothers, even though they could identify aspects of child care which seemed hard work.

However, Coyne sets these mother's experiences in the context of a society which, as she sees it, allows them no status. She adopts an 'ecological' approach:

> The ecological approach then examines the factors and the actors which form a dynamic system within a physical and social environment. For schoolgirl mothers this examination reveals: that they do not accurately perceive the social reality of under-16 pregnancy and motherhood; they do not adequately appreciate the potential results of sexual activity and have not internalised an 'at risk' role; they do not realise that biological maturity does not license activating this capacity at will, but with societal constraints; that the girls do not perceive the objective but only the subjective aspect of motherhood and further, once the baby is born, that it takes precedence over its mother in terms of societal protection and at the same time the mother loses her own privileged status as a child. (Coyne 1986 pp. 25–26)

What is striking in examining Coyne's work is that her theoretical perspective appears not to give full weight to the responses which she is given by the young mothers themselves. In fact, she dismisses their sense of competence and satisfaction in the role of motherhood as showing an 'inability to perceive the social reality of under-16 pregnancy and motherhood' and as perceiving only the 'subjective aspect of motherhood.' (Coyne 1986 pp. 25–26) This leads her to conclude that in spite of the positive views of the mothers themselves, her own knowledge of the objective disadvantages of being a young mother has more weight.

Coyne's key point is that mothers of school age no longer have the status of child and are not given by society the status of mother. Because she is working so hard to de-pathologize young mothers and put them in their social context in this way, I believe she omits to value how the young women themselves perceive the situation. Most of her sample who lived at home reported feeling comfortable at home, i.e. in the daughter/child role, but in addition enjoyed being treated as an adult. For the most part, the girls appeared to enjoy aspects of both statuses simultaneously and were anticipating a gradual move to physical separation from family.

Coyne is not the only researcher to have found an apparent contradiction between the objective circumstances of young mothers and their subjective account of their experiences. In their study, Simms and Smith (1985) interviewed 533 teenage mothers of whom ten were mothers of school age. They interviewed these younger mothers on two occasions:

> At the conclusion of the first set of interviews, when the babies were about four months old, we noted how cheerful the young mothers seemed about their future prospects. They thought the babies had improved the quality of their lives and could foresee no great problems in the near future. We wondered how far this seeming complacency was a reflection of the novelty of their situation.
>
> By the second interview, one year or more later, several of these young women had had severely adverse experiences. Nonetheless, most were still satisfied with their lives and their choices. (Simms and Smith 1986)

The authors are unable to explain the discrepancy that these positive responses highlight between the researchers' view of the mothers' circumstances and their own. They offer one or two possibilities. Perhaps these young mothers have to say they did the right thing 'in order to avoid feelings of dejection and failure.' Alternatively, if life offers little in other respects, perhaps having a baby, even when very young, has its compensations. This second idea certainly dominates Simms and Smith's view of those older teenage mothers in their study who they see as often becoming mothers for lack of other sources of self-esteem. Interestingly Boulton's study of older mothers, mentioned earlier, found that working-class mothers reported satisfaction with their role as mothers even though they experienced frustrations in providing care for children. Boulton suggests that 'satisfaction may well reflect only the less attractive alternatives they face rather than any more rewarding experience as such.' (Boulton 1983 p. 197)

These kind of statements are difficult to substantiate and are a dangerous route for a qualitative researcher to follow. If respondents report satisfaction with their role the researcher is in some difficulty if she suggests that this satisfaction is less 'real' than other kinds of satisfaction. If what is suggested is that women who have the opportunity to be doctors or lawyers would not so readily report satisfaction as mothers, does that diminish in any way the nature of the reported experience of these mothers who are satisfied with their role? Simms and Smith (1986) concluded rather differently saying that their interviews raised `all kinds of questions about how far it is ever possible to make judgements about the quality of people's lives.' (p. 119) Surely reporting people's own judgements about the quality of their lives is a reasonable starting point.

In addition to re-framing what school age mothers say about themselves some writers also redefine their behaviour and place it in a consistently negative light. Hudson and Ineichen (1991) having suggested that pregnant teenagers who decide to keep the baby are likely to be doing so for pathological reasons or because they are under duress, might be expected to paint a gloomy picture of motherhood:

> Many girls in their early teens take pregnancy in their stride, undergo a normal birth and assume motherhood in a fairly calm if slightly bewildered manner. Many others, however, do not. Both sorts of mother need help in different ways. The calmness of the first often belies the ignorance and inexpertise of their coping, while the childish, demanding behaviour of the second tells us how young they are and how desperate the situation is. (Hudson and Ineichen 1991 p. 114)

In fact, they can't win. However they present themselves, Hudson and Ineichen believe that there must be an underlying problem.

Hudson and Ineichen give examples of young women who have certainly got serious problems in their lives. They have known young mothers who have experienced rejection by their families and violence from the partners. They quote examples of young mothers in the care of the Local Authority who do not show commitment to the child and cannot cope with the responsibility. Some of the babies of these young mothers are said to have suffered neglect.

Although these are worrying stories it does seem that these young women generally suffered a range of problems prior to becoming mothers and that the problems experienced after the birth were not necessarily the result of their age. The severity of the problems involved in mothering a child is described as linked to a range of family, financial and housing problems. Although some aspects of these problems are age-related, poor housing, inadequate benefits and lack of child care must be seen as a failure in provision by the state. As Phoenix concludes of mothers under 20 generally, 'the problems they experience are attributed to age rather than to structural factors.' (Phoenix 1991b). In Phoenix's large sample, she found that teenage mothers were indeed concerned with how to cope with a low income. But equally, she found that their concern was entirely appropriate, in focusing on how best to feed, clothe and stimulate their children. (Phoenix 1991a)

The fact that some young mothers have experienced adverse circumstances within their own families is often quoted (Birch 1987, Hudson and Ineichen

1991) as a cause for concern in terms of the care the mother's own child will receive:

> Today's abused child is often a consequence of its parent's experience of abuse and is likely to be tomorrow's abusing parent. Deprivation and abuse can create a self-perpetuating cycle. (Hudson and Ineichen 1991 p. 161)

These statements need to be clarified in the light of the research literature on intergenerational links in parenting problems. When Quinton and Rutter (1988) reviewed the research they found that:

> In some circumstances there were striking intergenerational continuities in parenting breakdown; equally, however, it was clear that some individuals exposed to severely adverse patterns of child-rearing did not go on themselves to become poor parents. Both continuities and discontinuities needed to be explained. (Quinton and Rutter 1988)

Quinton and Rutter (1988) go on to suggest that although, for example, abusing mothers are more likely to have come from families where they had experienced substitute care or had experienced parental marital breakdown, the majority of mothers with adverse experiences did not abuse their children. The issues that need clarification are the extent to which there are factors which contribute to their 'resilience in the face of adversity' (Quinton and Rutter 1988 p. 19). This issue has not been well addressed in the literature on school age mothers but is essential in understanding them, acknowledging their strengths and considering whether there are factors which develop or build on coping mechanisms in the young mother. In the absence of accurate research, the references to a cycle of deprivation and even abuse merely contributes to a sense of helplessness and hopelessness in those who work with young mothers.

The long term consequences of early motherhood

There have been some challenges to the notion that early motherhood determines outcomes in all areas of life. Phoenix (1991a) in addition to challenging many of the negative assumptions that have been made about teenage mothers, found that:

> Women who become mothers early in their life courses are heterogeneous in a number of respects before they become mothers and heterogeneity is maintained after birth. (Phoenix 1991a p. 238)

Thus whatever themes or trends we identify, whether in terms of placing young mothers in a social context or finding numbers of mothers expressing satisfaction in their role, it is important to remember that the range of individual experiences – the ways in which each individual makes her choices and constructs her quality of life – is very wide.

This simple but fundamental idea is also a key finding of a longitudinal study carried out in the United States of mothers who gave birth as teenagers, seventeen years on. The follow up study by Furstenberg et al, *Adolescent Mothers in Later Life* (1987) found tremendous variation in outcomes. Although early child-bearers were disadvantaged in certain ways compared to their peers who have children later, 'the life course is sufficiently flexible to allow for a number of paths to recovery.' (Furstenberg et al. 1987 p. 75) He concludes that development in adult life, particularly when the young mother's child enters school, must be taken into account:

> The Baltimore study shows that many teen mothers stage a recovery in adulthood: They return to school after dropping out, find employment after a stay on welfare, and curtail fertility after one or two additional births. The time and sequencing of the life decisions that result in different life-course paths is often not set until after the first child has entered school and the mother has entered adulthood. This study highlights the fact that events occurring early in the lives of adolescent mothers are not the only ones to affect their later adjustment to parenthood. (Furstenberg et al. 1987 p. 152)

This is a particularly helpful idea because it locates the event of becoming a mother as just one part of development through the life-cycle. It need neither be seen as the end of a process, i.e. as an achievement of feminine identity (Erikson 1968) nor as the event which writes the women's life script for her and effectively ends all possibility of choice and independent fulfilment, as Campbell's widely quoted observation suggests:

> The girl who has an illegitimate child at the age of 16 suddenly has 90 per cent of her life's script written for her. Her life chances are few, and most of them are bad. (Campbell 1968 p. 238)

The variety of outcomes suggests a variety of factors which play a part in determining the experience of being a mother at an early age. It is surprising that this needs to be stressed; few people would expect that all mothers between the ages of say twenty-five and twenty-seven would share the same experience of motherhood. It seems likely that it is the fact that very young mothers are seen as deviant that tends to lead to attempts at labelling which include assumptions of common characteristics.

6 Services for school age mothers

The literature on service provision for school age mothers is limited. There have been two large scale surveys of provision across the country (Miles et al. (1979) and Dawson (1987)) but generally information available comes from the evaluation of individual units (e.g. Southwell (1985)) and from newspaper and journal articles which look at specific units and draw on the views of one or two mothers.

Although most reports focus on educational provision there has been one report which was concerned with the whole range of provision from health, education, social services and housing departments. (Miles et al. (1979)) This report arose from a study undertaken by members of a Joint Working Party:

> The Working Party started from the assumption that pregnancy in schoolgirls is in general so stressful and so full of risks to both mother and child that society has a responsibility to ensure that wherever possible it should be avoided. However, some girls will become pregnant whatever the prevailing attitudes and whatever the policies and practices for prevention. It is therefore necessary to ensure that the lives of individual girls, their babies and the babies' fathers are not ruined and that the best outcome is achieved for them all. Urgent consideration and action are needed to minimize health risks to mother and child, loss of education, emotional distress and isolation, financial hardship and the dilemmas and confusion created by existing legislation. This would surely be for the benefit of society as well as for the individuals concerned. (Miles 1979 p. 8)

Although the Working Party's brief was to examine services, describing the experience of girls who became pregnant at school was a necessary first step. The method chosen was to contact a sample of schools across the country and ask Head teachers to complete detailed questionnaires about girls who had become pregnant at school in the last three years. Although the questionnaires asked for a great deal of information about each girl's family background as well as educational circumstances, this information would seem to have been provided by the school without the involvement of the girls themselves. Apart from the fact that it seems unlikely that schools would have such details, it means that only the most basic facts can be ascertained. Some of these are then used as the basis for a degree of speculation about the attitudes of the girls. For example:

> Our survey data can be seen to suggest that girls and their parents do see schools as sympathetic and understanding. When schools learned of a pregnancy they were most likely to be told of it by the girl herself and/or her parents. (Miles 1979 p. 24)

It seems inevitable that girls or their parents would need to inform the school of the pregnancy so to suggest that this is evidence that the schools are seen as sympathetic and understanding is unwarranted. In fact they found that 75 per cent had left school by the 5th month of pregnancy and 60 per cent of these girls received no education between leaving school and the birth. (Miles et al. 1979) Thus a significant number of young mothers were falling through the net as far as education was concerned during pregnancy.

A more recent survey (Dawson 1987) found that the variation in the provision of education for young mothers after the birth was a particular cause for concern. Her findings were that although home tuition was generally available during pregnancy it was not always offered in the postnatal period. In addition, group tuition was not well established and where it was available not all offered a nursery or creche facility. (See Table 6.1)

Table 6.1: 1987 Survey – Metropolitan and non-metropolitan districts of England and Wales

	Metropolitan	Non-Metropolitan
No. of districts in England and Wales	57	48
Replies to 1987 survey	32	32
(i) with information	29	31
(ii) without information	3	1
Home tuition		
(i) no provision	3	0
(ii) provision of home tuition	26	31
(iii) during antenatal period alone	5	10
(iv) during both antenatal and postnatal periods	21	19
(v) period not specified/on ad hoc basis	0	2
Group tuition		
(i) no provision	12	16
(ii) provision of special centre or established group provision		
(a) with nursery/creche	10	7
(b) without nursery/creche	4	4
(iii) ad hoc group provision (without nursery/creche)	3	4

Source: Dawson, 1987

These figures, according to Dawson, conceal quite a variation between education authorities, with one authority having five centres and other authorities having only one centre.

Miles et al. (1979) found that young mothers also tended to be disadvantaged in terms of social security benefits and housing. They were excluded because of their age from benefits available to other single parents which created an impossible situation for young women, whether they were depending on their parents or were trying to become independent. The situation regarding benefits has not improved since this report was produced and must be seen as an additional source of stress.

Area Health Authorities and Social Services Departments were found to be unaware of the special needs of this group, whether it was in the area of antenatal care or the provision of counselling and support. Miles et al. were unable to determine from the information available whether it was the girls themselves who did not feel comfortable in groups of older mothers and therefore did not take up the services that could be helpful to them. The report concluded that:

Pregnant schoolgirls are a group with special health needs. Ante-natal care ... should be given separately from that given to older and married women. (Miles et al. 1979 p. 20)

To meet the girl's emotional needs, they recommended that:

Social Services Departments and voluntary agencies should encourage the establishment of more supportive groups which give young mothers the opportunity to meet together for mutual help and shared activities. (Miles et al. 1979 p. 30)

The report has two key messages. First, that given the range of circumstances among this group of young women and the range of services which need to be available from different agencies, there should be a co-ordinated approach:

At local level there should be a designation of persons with special responsibility at management level in education, health, social services, and housing and in any relevant voluntary agency. There should be someone to act as co-ordinator and this might most appropriately be the Specialist in Community Medicine (Child Health). (Miles et al. 1979 p. 46)

Secondly, the Working Party's focus for intervention was to enable the girl's life to be as normal as possible:

The guiding principle of provision relating to schoolgirl pregnancies should be to enable families wherever possible to solve their own dilemmas with the minimum of stress and hardship. (p. 46)

This emphasis on normalising the girl's experience led the group to conclude that although special units have some advantages, it was preferable for young women to return to school:

The advantages of these units are their links with other services, their high staffing ratios and their flexible approach. But we believe that those positive aspects are outweighed by their disadvantages. These include the risk of stigma; an unnecessarily long time off school; difficulties in returning to school because of lost contact with friends, and the break with the school's education programme. (p. 26)

It should be remembered that those conclusions were based on the views of a number of professionals and the research did not include the views of the young mothers themselves. Miles et al. did not underestimate the importance of contact between young mothers for mutual support but saw this as occurring in groups organised separately from education.

Southwell, examining the work of a unit in Bradford, found that the unit did have some limitations. She found in particular that more academic girls were unlikely to get their educational needs met. The absence of a range of specialist subject teachers, the absence of appropriate library facilities and the absence of a peer group working for the same exams are mentioned. (Southwell 1985 p. 50) She also found that because of the emphasis on education in child care, the unit was not suitable for a pregnant girl who was planning to give up the baby for adoption.

However, she noted certain benefits of the unit. The level of attendance at the unit was impressive, particularly given the history of truancy by some of the girls. The girls benefited from being in a caring environment where they were treated as young adults rather than children and appeared to mature as a result. Southwell draws a wider conclusion from this:

> This points to the case for schools to think about the ways their social and educational organisation meets the needs of fast maturing young people. (Southwell 1985 p. 47)

Dawson (1987), Sharpe (1987) and Coyne (1986) all disagree with the conclusion of Miles et al. (1979) that the disadvantages of small units outweigh the advantages:

> At their best, special centres for pregnant schoolgirl mothers may have the following features:
>
> – health care is ensured
>
> – counselling on such matters as contraception and personal relationships is available
>
> – girls can receive mutual support from each other and experienced staff
>
> – as well as the opportunity to follow academic subjects a girl can follow essential parentcraft and child-care programmes
>
> – information on finances (e.g. DHSS benefits) and teaching on how to manage money, with courses on home management can be available.
>
> – liaison with other agencies (careers service, health and social service agencies) can be made available
>
> – provision of nursery facilities enables a girl to continue her education and be close to her baby.' (Dawson 1987)

Sharpe (1987) and Coyne (1986) share Dawson's view that it is the combination of support and education which they feel can best be achieved at a special unit. Coyne suggests that this helps the girl bridge the gap between schoolgirl and mother. (Coyne p. 22) Sharpe and Coyne both included interviews with the young mothers in their research.

Although units have been viewed positively in the recent literature the concerns expressed by Miles et al. (1979) and Southwell (1985) are not fully answered. In particular the need to ensure that academically able young women are not disadvantaged by their attendance at a unit must be addressed.

Other units also accept that this is a risk. (Arbour Project – Personal communication 1991) The issue has not been given a high profile because on the whole the units at least allow some form of education to continue up to the birth and after the birth which is generally seen as an improvement on the past. There is also a danger of low expectations because some pregnant girls are very behind with their school work when they come to the unit and basic skills may become the focus for the whole group.

In addition the question of whether services unnecessarily isolate pregnant schoolgirls from other young women needs to be considered. Miles et al. (1979) expressed some concern about this. It is an issue which can be seen as part of the broader debate about whether children with special needs should be accommodated within the normal school system or benefit most from specialist provision. This is an issue which will be considered in Part III of this book but for the moment it is worth mentioning one unusual unit which has been praised in the recent literature (Hudson and Ineichen 1991) and in the media – the unit at Wester Hailes in Scotland.

This unit exists within a community school which offers education to any member of the community. Because of this, there is a creche in existence for the children of mothers of all ages. As elsewhere in the country, the unit started as a result of a home tutor seeing the need to bring pregnant schoolgirls together. It was established in 1986 and teaches five girls at a time just before and after the baby is born. They are joined by five mothers over the age of 16. Beyond this period of time they are integrated into normal classes. Smith (1989) suggests that this is the only unit of its kind in Britain and that its success depends very much on the ethos of a community school. In addition, the teacher when interviewed by Smith indicated that she found that the small size of the group was important in enabling individual attention to be paid to the needs of each girl. (Smith 1990) Thus the unit responds flexibly to their needs and provides the benefit of a small, friendly group but also operates within a large and complex institution with a wide range of resources.

The provision of groups for pregnant girls and young mothers outside of an educational framework has been attempted in various forms ranging from therapeutic groups (Cant 1980) to youth work projects. Writers conclude that young mothers are difficult to motivate to attend groups and this is echoed in the American literature (Miller 1983). Persuading young women to attend antenatal classes even specifically for their age group is also hard, although persistence can lead to successful groups (Evans and Parker 1985).

Where groups may prove effective is in circumstances in which the young mothers have other shared concerns. Groups for single black mothers in Handsworth, Birmingham, were found to meet a range of needs, for example support in coping with racism in housing policy and social security offices, in addition to support as a mother. (Davies 1983) It seems that getting young mothers together simply as young mothers may not be as effective as attaching support and counselling to other provisions, which is why tuition units may have advantages.

Although there has been some gathering of information about the availability of differing kinds of provision, there has been little comparative study of the success of different resources. Coyne (1986) interviewed young mothers in different circumstances, ranging from those in a residential unit to those unsupported in the community. She concluded that specialist units were necessary to 'develop and maximise the girls' potential as mothers and students.' (Coyne 1986 p. 24) However, Coyne does not define success and this would appear to be a common difficulty for researchers. Does success mean the best outcome for the mother, the baby, the mother's family? Should it be judged in educational, emotional or social terms? Are there differences in the long and the short term? How can such measures be established for such a diverse group?

It is not possible to tackle these major issues in the context of this research project, but perhaps two questions stand out in relation to service provision. First, how can specialist provision be offered to meet the specific needs of these girls while at the same time helping them to lead as normal a life as possible, avoiding in particular stigma and isolation? Secondly, how can channels be provided for young mothers themselves to influence the nature of services and to be empowered to make choices?

7 A problem to themselves or a problem to society? The role of ideology

Having dealt with the literature related to the experiences of school age mothers and the services available to them, it is important to step back a little and draw together some of the issues which are contained in that literature and which suggest processes at work at the level of ideology.

The fact that society has a role in defining school age mothers in a particular way is apparent from the sense in which they are viewed as a social problem. This, as was suggested in the Preface, is the message in the Government White Paper on health but is also apparent, for example, in the way in which the Social Security Benefits system refuses to acknowledge the needs of young mothers for financial support. These are ways by which the otherwise private behaviour of sexual relationships, pregnancy and motherhood are brought into the public domain and defined by cultural images and by the responses of key agencies in society. Isolated examples in the media of young mothers coping well with their children have not shifted the underlying discomfort about 'children' as mothers. As Murcott puts it:

> Teenage pregnancy as a problem may then be understood as a matter of social pollution, located at the intersection of ideologies of reproduction on one hand and ideologies of childhood on the other. (Murcott 1980)

By this formulation, Murcott seeks to challenge the idea that labelling teenage pregnancy as a problem is 'common-sense'. Given that she sees the ideology of childhood as fundamental to an understanding of attitudes towards teenage pregnancy in general, the impact of that ideology on attitudes towards mothers of school age must be seen as even more significant.

A key element, Murcott suggests, in understanding the idea of school age pregnancy as a social problem lies in the premise that the welfare of children will dictate the future welfare of society. This is an established part of our view of how society maintains itself, generally seen as the process of childhood socialization. Although that process has always been the subject of debate, the principle that is at stake is that of the transmission of norms and values. The aspect of the child's welfare which is most likely to matter is her behaviour and her moral welfare. Child mothers are seen to breach a whole range of moral and social boundaries: they are evidence of sexual activity below the age of consent; they are supposedly too young to mother; they are unmarried; they are likely to depend on benefits and need housing by the state and so on. In themselves they represent a whole collection of what are deemed to be problems. Although they might be thought to invite sympathy as victims of circumstances or even victims of men, they are more likely to be seen as morally flawed and therefore in themselves and through their children as a source of contamination.

As Murcott points out, young mothers are the focus of professional concern for aspects of their welfare. The medical world in particular takes a special interest in both children and reproduction. Children and pregnant women are not the subject of medical attention because they are ill and yet the process of special screening marks them out as an 'at risk' population. This is, as the Court Report title indicates, because children need to be 'fit' so that the nation can be 'Fit for the Future.' (Court 1976)

Thus concerns about the child/adult ambiguity which school age mothers represent takes on a much broader significance when both the mothers and their children are seen in medical and moral terms as breaching the normal code and therefore storing up problems for society as a whole. The fear of social pollution (see Douglas (1970) for further exposition of this concept) has been the source of stigma and oppression for different groups of reproductive women throughout history. The stigma of illegitimacy has only recently lessened. As Howe et al. (1992) demonstrate, many unmarried women felt such fear for themselves and their children even twenty years ago that they gave their babies up for adoption. Mothers of illegitimate babies who did not give up their babies for adoption were labelled as having psychological and social problems which led them to the misguided decision to keep the child. More recently single mothers, whether previously married or not, have become a convenient group to which many of society's ills can be attributed. Now we also have as the target young mothers, whose babies are born illegitimate and who are likely to remain single parents for a period after the birth because of their age. They too are labelled, if they choose to keep their babies, as doing so for range of psychological and social reasons which reflect adversely on their decision.

Being seen as a social problem is merely the starting point for a range of negative stereotypes, some of which are reflected in the literature. In 1977, MacIntyre listed a comparison between assumptions made about married and unmarried mothers. With acknowledgements to MacIntyre (1977), it is possible to generate an only slightly modified comparison between school age mothers and older mothers.

For mothers of average childbearing age

1. Pregnancy and childbearing are normal and desirable, and conversely a desire not to have at least some children is aberrant and in need of explanation.

2. Pregnancy and childbearing are not problematic and for a woman to treat them as such indicates that she is not normal.

3. Children of a mother over the age of 20 should not be surrendered for adoption unless in exceptional circumstances.

4. The loss of a baby by miscarriage, stillbirth or neonatal death will occasion deep instinctive distress and grief.

For school age mothers

1. Pregnancy and childbearing are abnormal and undesirable.

2. Pregnancy and childbearing are problematic and for a young woman not to treat them as such is unusual and in need of psychological or social explanations.

3. It is usually best for the pregnancy to be terminated or the baby to be given up for adoption. A woman who wishes to keep her child is unrealistic, selfish, lacking in ambition or emotionally needy.

4. The loss of a baby by abortion, miscarriage, stillbirth or neonatal death should not occasion too much distress or grief and may produce relief.

8   Conclusion

The literature on school age mothers describes a group of young women who have not on the whole chosen to be pregnant but having become pregnant have taken on the responsibilities of motherhood. The process of becoming a mother at an early age can leave them vulnerable to a range of stresses. The source of these stresses is regularly described in terms of loss of educational and career opportunities, health problems, family conflicts and problems with money and housing. Although these disadvantages may be associated with the age of the mothers, there is no evidence that age would continue to be decisive if various Government and local authority departments were to respond more appropriately to the specific needs of young mothers.

The emphasis on chronological age affects service provision but says nothing about the range of potential for becoming successful mothers. Melhuish and Phoenix (1987) reviewing the literature noted 'the relative lack of attention paid to the enormous diversity of people who fall within an arbitrary age criterion'.

The source of stress which could be most difficult of all to tackle is that which emerges from the negative stereotyping referred to above, which has an impact on how young women maintain their self-esteem. There is a need to explore not just the circumstances of young mothers or even how society views them but to listen to how young mothers themselves talk about their experiences and how they make sense of the transition to motherhood. As Hudson and Ineichen (1991) put it:

> It is impossible for teenagers to control the discourse about themselves and very difficult sometimes for them just to get a hearing. (p. 225)

In Part II one group of school age mothers' views will be reported and analysed to establish more detail about their experiences, perceptions and attitudes.

48

Part II
THE EXPERIENCE OF PREGNANCY, BIRTH AND MOTHERHOOD: SCHOOL AGE MOTHERS TELL THEIR STORY

Part II

9 Methodology

Planning a research strategy

Although there was a mass of literature which might contribute to an enhanced understanding of young mothers, there was a relatively limited amount of material specifically relating to girls who become pregnant while still at school. Of this material, there was a mix of statistical information, theoretical frameworks and some use of interview material with the young women themselves. As the conclusion of the literature survey suggested, the use made of interview material was often rather dubious with researchers taking the step of discrediting certain kinds of statements on the basis that the researcher judged them to be unrealistic, immature, desperate, or defensive (Coyne 1986, Hudson and Ineichen 1991). It can be seen that the need to interview young mothers was therefore recognised but that as a group they presented particular difficulties to researchers who were reluctant to give due weight to their views and tended to impose their own value judgements. It seemed important for the purposes of this current research to clarify the nature of those difficulties before embarking on the interviews.

One of the dilemmas for a researcher in this area reflects the dilemmas experienced by the young people themselves. At its simplest, should these young mothers be seen as children or as adults? If they are children, then it is sometimes anticipated that adults can appropriately speak for them, defining them and their characteristics. Some research methodologies have included direct contact between the researchers and their child subjects, (e.g. Thoburn et al. 1986). Indeed, Thoburn et al. commented on the necessary but difficult process for social workers of using the expressed views of children as a basis for planning. (Thoburn et al. 1986, p. 180) It seems possible that for researchers too, the contributions of child subjects to research about them may need careful handling. However, it may be that by virtue of their age, i.e. 15 years and over, young mothers can be seen as young adults. Perhaps it is the fact that they are mothers that should give them adult status. In any event, their views need to be heard. This is the position taken by Phoenix (1991) in her book, *Young Mothers?* She was interviewing teenage women of 16 and above and to her it was an important part of the project that their expressed views should be respected and she works hard not to discredit them in reporting them. The message of the Children Act 1989 has been that listening to young people must become central to understanding their needs and taking on board their wishes and feelings.

This leads on to another important area in considering the use of interviews with young women; not their age, but their gender. The material on feminist research (Roberts 1981, Wilkinson 1986, Skevington and Baker 1989) has presented a case for believing that:

> ... women's experiences contribute a different view of reality, an entirely different 'ontology' or way of going about making sense of the world. (Stanley and Wise p. 117 in Wilkinson ed. 1986)

Oakley (1981) has suggested that women are often neglected in research studies and that sociology and psychology have often been guilty of accepting a patriarchal definition of women's experiences. For her, therefore, it was important to listen to what women have to say and record it faithfully. This process is not, however, as simple as it may sound and Oakley's views on the nature of the interview – the heart of the process – have been the subject of critical debate (e.g. Malseed 1987, Ribbens 1989) which merits further attention. Hearing the 'different voices' of women, as Gilligan (1982) describes them, involves developing a strategy for listening. Oakley suggests that there are traditional criteria for interviewing which arise from the interview being seen as an information gathering tool. She goes on to say that there is an often stated need for 'rapport':

> 'Rapport', a commonly used but ill-defined term, does not mean in this context what the dictionary says it does ('a sympathetic relationship', OED) but the acceptance by the interviewee of the interviewer's research goals and the interviewee's active search to help the interviewer in providing the relevant information. The person who is interviewed has a passive role in adapting to the definition of the situation offered by the person doing the interviewing. The person doing the interviewing must actively and continually construct the 'respondent' (a telling name) as passive. (Oakley 1981 p. 35)

Oakley sees herself as taking on an entirely different role as interviewer when interviewing women as mothers. (Oakley 1981). She describes establishing a relationship with the women interviewed by offering information in response to questions about herself, helping with the housework and being present at the birth of their babies. She reports with some satisfaction that a number of the women became close friends and appears to see this as evidence of achieving a successful level of reciprocity in the interview situation.

Ribbens (1989) queries Oakley's claim of achieving reciprocity. She puts the question, 'How do we then acknowledge our power, and yet deal with feminist concerns with intimacy, reciprocity, and collaboration?' Ribbens points out that Oakley was only asked on average 1.2 questions per interview that were classified as personal, advice questions or questions about the research. Given the flow of personal information from the interviewee, this is hardly reciprocity. She also comments that Oakley in writing up her research risks being influenced by the close friendships which she established and that the privacy and confidentiality which she offered belies the public nature of a research enterprise. Ribbens suggests that far from being a positive outcome of interviewing, the continuing relationship reflects a difficulty that women researchers have in coping with a situation which is confusing in its social construction:

> It is likely that it is precisely because women researchers are particularly sensitive to the possibility that the interviewee has been asked to expose themselves in a manner that normally occurs within long term caring relationships, that makes them uneasy about leaving interviewees. (Ribbens 1989 p. 588)

For Ribbens and Oakley, there are assumed differences in the interview situation which arise from the fact that both the interviewee and the interviewer are women. Oakley frames this in terms of the shared experiences of the participants; Ribbens refers to the 'particular sensitivities' of a woman researcher. Although this is part of a wider issue about the relevance of the sex of the interviewer, for me, embarking on research as a woman interviewing women, I was keen to bear in mind the possible advantages and risks in the situation.

One fairly fundamental point which emerges from this debate is that however closely we plan to report the words of women, the researcher's involvement in the face to face encounter of an interview will affect the nature of the outcome and therefore the substance of the research. Oakley describes her role as 'being a data collecting instrument for those whose lives are being researched.' I find Ribbens' view more persuasive:

> Perhaps we have to take responsibility for ourselves, recognise that in the end we are not data collecting instruments for anyone, but are data creating social beings and acknowledge our own presence within the accounts we give of other people's lives. (Ribbens 1989 p. 590)

This does not mean that we should not aim to reflect faithfully the views and feelings of those we interview; it does mean that we must acknowledge and be aware of the choices we make and the impact we have as researchers.

In anticipating my own research interviews, I had to consider the undeniable baggage which I would bring with me. As a woman, as a mother, as an older person of a certain race, a certain class with a certain accent and a certain style of dress, it was not hard to anticipate that my presence in a young mother's living room would have an impact over and beyond my definition of the situation which arose from the research focus. As Ribbens (1989) puts it, such interviews are 'complex social encounters.'

It was then necessary to consider this particular group of women who were to be interviewed in order to understand these encounters further. Although there was some variation in age and situation, they shared an experience which had been potentially a source of stigma. In addition, a number were unemployed, single parents, and living on benefits. Most obvious of all was the fact that they were women. Such factors combined, in my view, to suggest that the interview process could be experienced as objectifying them, as feeding into the sense that they were generally powerless and in addition were being treated as deviant, as oddities who were being interviewed mainly as a result of their unusual behaviour. It seemed that enabling these particular young women to tell their story was complicated by a range of power imbalances between interviewer and interviewee which went beyond those which are inevitable because of the nature of the research situation.

In addition the role of the interviewer and the interviewee could not be clarified without regard to the subjects under discussion. As Oakley (1979) found in interviewing women about childbirth, the emotive nature of the content, the anxiety and the vulnerability of the women, can lead to a situation in which the interviewer is looked to for reassurance and even for information.

It was inevitable that, as with Oakley's research, interviewing young mothers was likely to produce intensely personal material relating to sexuality, family life, their role as mothers, the development of their children and so on. Ribbens (1989) suggests that interviewing mothers about motherhood was particularly intense because the role of mother is 'an over-arching and organising status, and this tends to lead mothers to relate to each other as whole people rather than within specific and instrumental roles.' (Ribbens 1989 p. 588)

To deal with this dilemma, it seemed possible that social work practice itself might have something to offer, since there too consideration has to be given to a very similar range of issues, i.e.

(i) the way in which the worker imposes their definition of the situation on the client.

(ii) the impact of the worker's and the client's own class, sex, race, personal history and resources on the exchange between worker and client.

(iii) the professional/personal conflict for the worker in maintaining boundaries in the face of emotive areas of discussion and the parallel conflict for the client in giving trust and yet maintaining appropriate defences.

The fact that the interviewer and the interviewee share the experience of being a woman and a mother may put them to some extent in the same relationship to a patriarchal society and the interviewer may feel able to share the perspective of the interviewee. The school age mothers of my sample still represented a challenge to the researcher in terms of being able to enter their world.

One of the models that social work practice, and particularly feminist social work practice, has generated to deal with the dilemmas of any interview situation is that of partnership and empowerment. The young women who were the focus of my research were parents who had had their children at an early age. Although still young at the time of interview it was important to enable them to feel that they were participating as valued individuals in a co-operative venture; thus neither objectifying them for scientific purposes nor falsely assuming a common experience. As discussed earlier, this does not mean denying the issues of power but it does suggest a framework which allows interviewees some sense of control in the interview process and some satisfaction that their views are being sought and valued. It was hoped that the research would be seen by these young mothers as an opportunity both to influence potentially the future of the tuition unit and to set the record straight in terms of the perceived stereotypes and that this would be in itself rewarding.

Although obtaining the material can be seen as a complex process, it is then necessary to analyse that material in such a way as to draw useful conclusions from it. For this process I turned to the model of grounded theory. (Strauss 1987) This style of qualitative analysis of data deals with the question of 'how to capture the complexity of the reality (phenomena) we study and how to make convincing sense of it.' (Strauss 1987 p. 10)

Strauss goes on to suggest that it is necessary to do 'detailed, intensive microscopic examination of the data in order to bring out the amazing complexity of what lies in, behind, and beyond those data.' (Strauss 1987 p. 10)

For my purposes, the examination of the data took several forms. Initially listening to the tapes and getting a sense of the feelings involved was important. From there, isolating the themes that were emerging involved very different elements – certain events, certain kinds of relationships, certain people and agencies in their environment which made a difference. It was these elements which structured the presentation of the interview material in Part II. It was necessary then to generate concepts which would be helpful in analysing the material and in turn generate theories about young mothers. In the event the theories needed to explain both the interview material and the literature. The literature is part of the data that must be taken into account. This is not simply because of the explicit content of other research but because attitudes revealed by researchers and writers appeared to represent a range of views in society that contribute to the environment which the girls face. As Strauss points out (Strauss 1989 p. 3) the research materials are not only the interviews but one must look to a range of elements. In this case the law, the education system, values expressed in the media, all help in generating theories which are of assistance in making sense of the world of young mothers.

From this point I hoped to go beyond the theories which assist understanding to considering ways forward in terms of principles for future services for young mothers. This very practical step is not a feature of all qualitative research but as a social worker, concerned with the welfare of such a potentially vulnerable group, this was equally important. This then forms the substance of Part III.

The study group

In Ipswich as elsewhere in the country, the initiative for developing a special provision for pregnant school girls and mothers of school age came from a single teacher. The provision of a special unit arose from a home tutor having the idea of grouping together pregnant girls receiving home tuition. Up until the tuition unit was set up in Ipswich in 1982, pregnant school girls would be offered home tuition of around 4 hours a week. After the baby was born, the tuition may have continued or, if the girl had a family member able to care for the child, she might have chosen to return to school. Nationally the picture has been that school age mothers often do not continue in education after the birth (Dawson 1987) and it seems likely that this was so in Ipswich, although there are no records to confirm this.

From the beginning, the intention of the tutor in bringing two pregnant school girls together was not predominantly for educational reasons but because she felt that the girls needed to share some of their feelings and concerns with someone else in the same situation. This basic principle has continued alongside the development of the educational aims for the unit.

Since its establishment in a family centre run by the Ormiston Trust the unit has become the central resource for pregnant school girls and school aged mothers in Ipswich and the surrounding area. The numbers on register have varied, with 12 girls in any one year being the maximum. As of January 1991, the total who had attended the unit was 55. The expectation is that each girl will attend from 9.30 am to 2.30 pm on two days a week with a maximum group of 4 attending at any one time. There is flexibility around the number of attendances per week depending on the stage of the pregnancy, the number of examination subjects and the social situation of the mother. A young mother in a homeless families unit, for example, might be invited to attend more often.

From the point at which the pregnancy becomes known to the school, the education welfare officer will make a referral to the unit. The assessment at this stage is largely of the young woman's educational needs and how they can be met within the unit. Neither the school, the education welfare service, nor the unit see themselves as having a role in counselling as regards the outcome of the pregnancy.

There is normally a preliminary meeting between the girl, her parents or carers, the unit staff and the Education Welfare Officer. There are no specific guidelines as to at which stage in the pregnancy the young woman will start to attend the unit and this is dependent on circumstances. Attendance continues up until the birth of the child and has included sitting examinations on the day the baby is due on occasions.

The girls study a core curriculum of mathematics, English and child care. Beyond this, the range of subjects taken has depended on the interest and ability of the young person, the teaching skills of the tutor and the co-operation of the school in allowing a return there for specific subjects, such as science. Other home tutors have also offered tuition in certain subjects. The range of educational levels achieved has been considerable, with some girls attaining fairly basic literacy and numeracy skills, while others move on to study at 'A' level within the unit.

In addition to the education programme, there is a series of sessions covering antenatal preparation which includes advice on welfare rights, first aid, etc. as well as information regarding pregnancy, childbirth and care of the new baby.

From discussions with the unit teacher, it became apparent that it is the interface between the educational needs of school girls and the emotional and practical needs of young mothers that presents the fundamental challenge to her skills. As referred to earlier, research both here and in the United States has stressed both the potential damage caused by the interruption which pregnancy causes to the girl's education but also the emotional vulnerability of the young mother and consequent concerns for her child. The young mothers often only attend the tuition unit for a few months and generally for a relatively few hours in a week. Yet this is a time when research on mothers of any age, (e.g. Oakley 1979, Boulton 1983) suggests that there is a crisis of transition. For these young women, the normal adolescent stress of taking examinations, considering careers and beginning to separate from parents is handled simultaneously with taking on the role of a mother. There are many powerful feelings at work in the group at any one time.

The sample

Although the nature of this research was qualitative, it was decided that it would be useful to adopt a simple stratified random sampling method to select which of the young women should be interviewed. Thus the names were put in year order of attendance at the unit and every third name was taken. It was of interest to consider experiences over a range of years – not so much to see whether the unit had changed essentially but to explore whether up to eight years on, the women's reflections on the experience would shed further light on the meaning it held for them. As described in Part I, Furstenberg's long-term follow up study in the United States has been particularly influential in re-evaluating some of the assumptions previously made about young mothers. (Furstenberg 1987)

All of the young women in the sample were white. There have been black girls attending the unit but they have been a very small minority. The absence of young mothers from different cultural and racial backgrounds must be accepted as a limitation of this research and would need to be addressed in any larger research programme.

The interview format

It was necessary to devise an interview format suitable for the semi-structured interviews which seemed appropriate for this group. It was important to have the kind of framework which would assist me in guiding the young women through the topics that needed to be covered and yet enabling them to tell their own story. One of the goals of the research was to examine the ways in which young women put their own pattern of meaning on their experiences and develop their own language for explaining experiences to themselves so it was central that the interviews should be able to flow easily. The need for some kind of structure in the interview arose from the themes identified in the literature survey: what was the young woman's view of each stage of the transition to motherhood and what were the key factors affecting the woman's experiences? The framework for this part of the research project was therefore an attempt to bring together the chronology of the experience with the factors which may have had an impact at each stage. (See Figure 9.1.)

	The young woman's own reactions	Father of the baby	Parents	School	Tuition unit	Others
Pregnancy						
Birth						
Motherhood						

Figure 9.1: The interview framework

The interview format therefore identified areas which would be covered in general terms but on the basis that each young woman would have their own particular interests and their own points of reference which would dictate the details of each interview.

Conducting the interviews

Having identified eighteen women whom I wished to interview, I wrote to each one. I was aware that in the Thomas Coram study of teenage mothers, it could take as many as ten visits to complete a successful interview, (Phoenix

1991), but although there were some difficulties, my sample group were mainly at home as arranged.

One young woman had left the area. Three others were not at home on several occasions and it was not possible to establish whether they had moved. Two more contacted me to say they did not wish to participate. I selected two more names from the list and in the end interviewed thirteen young women. Of these, two were pregnant and currently at the Unit, so I interviewed them while pregnant and subsequently after the baby was born. The interviews took place in the young women's homes except for those currently at the unit.

As I took each person through the chronology of events, I found that several preferred to tell the story in the order that made sense to them. For some this meant talking in detail about the present, because current issues were preoccupying them and needed to be covered first. Others went to the birth itself very rapidly and having described that, were then happy to reflect on school, the pregnancy etc. My interventions, questions, or prompts, were variously followed to the letter, gently ignored or roundly rejected. It was not my role to provide a therapeutic outlet in any sense and I was careful never to challenge an interviewee to go more deeply into her emotions than she would readily offer. On two occasions, cups of coffee were made to create a diversion after significant events were recounted. This occurred, for example, after telling me of the cot death of a baby, and the break down of a relationship.

In addition the presence or absence of the child of the early pregnancy affected the nature of the interaction. In all cases though I asked about the child's welfare. If the child was not present, I was generally shown a photograph and it seemed important to the women to 'introduce' their child to me.

There was no doubt that the interviews with the older women contrasted greatly with the interviews with those still at the Unit with small babies. This was inevitable but nevertheless it was helpful to see the ways in which women reflected on what their hopes had been at 15 and the successes they had achieved since. If I had interviewed them at 15 I may have been tempted to see their ambitions as immature and unrealistic.

The young women were willing to talk in some detail and with great emotion about their experiences. They generally offered ideas and opinions which went beyond the questions asked. This suggested that they had thought long and hard over the years about that point in their lives when they found out they were pregnant and when they became mothers. Each person wanted to ensure that I understood what it had really been like for them. The interview material which follows illustrates both the range of different experiences and the connections or shared themes that emerged. This section draws on the words of these young women and the quotations reflect as accurately as possible the language which they used to describe their experiences. The tone of voice and the feelings behind the words are harder to capture in print but it is hoped that some sense of these young women and the meaning they attached to pregnancy, birth and motherhood does emerge.

10 Pregnancy

Although all the young women were in very different circumstances at the time they became pregnant, the realisation that they were pregnant represented a crisis in all their lives. At this turning point, there was a need for the young women to come to terms with the very different view that others would now have of them and the very different view that they must now have of themselves; all of this alongside a whole range of practical implications which they would have to face.

This section will capture some of the experiences which characterised the pregnancies of these young mothers and will consider the ways in which their own personal resources and the key figures in their lives affected their ability to accommodate the idea of the pregnancy and their ability to cope with its consequences.

The mother's own reactions

None of the mothers interviewed described the pregnancy as in any way planned. All of the girls had been in a relationship with the father of the baby at the time of conception, although Wendy and the father of her baby had been 'just friends' and she became pregnant the first time she had sex:

> We were very good friends. That's all we were literally just friends. We used to hang about together ... It started to develop, just kissy, kissy, cuddle, cuddle and then before I knew it, it was too late ... It was a couple of kids fooling about and with all the best intentions, he was only sixteen, three seconds maximum and that's it and it was too late.

For Wendy, the pregnancy cut right across her plans for herself. She was in top sets at school and was looking forward to a career as a graphic designer:

I was never going to get married, never going to have children. I was going to live in a nice big penthouse flat and have a career ... I'm selfish – I like doing what I want to do and because I'm always right I have to do it my way ... I know what my bad points are, put it that way!

Given that context it would not have been surprising if Wendy had had to think long and hard as to whether she was going to keep the baby. However:

My Mum gave me all the options but I'd already made up my mind to keep it. Being me I'm pretty adamant, once I make up my mind anyway. I knew I would keep it. I knew – but I don't know why. I don't have any maternal instincts but I just knew I had to keep it.

It seems that the determination and drive which was to go into achieving the penthouse flat was directed into the decision to keep the baby, against the odds.

For Emma too the fact of her pregnancy at 14 seemed the end of her ambitions. She was academically bright and was looking towards 'A' levels and some form of college education:

I'd looked at a career book and I'd thought, when I was 28 I'd have two children. You know, the way you do, you stereotype yourself. 'I'm going to be a career woman'. I went through a phase of art college, then I wanted to be a social worker and then I went to Ipswich Hospital because I wanted to work in a lab ... We used contraceptives at first but then you just don't think about it. You just think it's not going to happen. It's so stupid I know. I just thought it would be impossible.

For Emma, there was the need to maintain some self-esteem in the face of what she felt was potential criticism of her, both for having a sexual relationship and for getting pregnant. She does this by referring to the fact that at least she had a proper relationship with the baby's father, unlike other girls:

It's like me in my position. I've said it so many times, *they're* always the ones who get away with it. Mine was a relationship. I know I shouldn't have been but again you get friends who have lots of relationships but they seem to get away with it.

Annette, too, felt some embarrassment both at the idea that she had had a sexual relationship at an early age and had not used contraception:

Now I look back the reason I got pregnant was because I was too scared to go to my Mum and say can I go on the pill, because I didn't want her knowing what I was doing. That's silly I know but that's the way I thought at the time and plus I think I was a bit ignorant. I just didn't think it would happen to me.

When she first realised she was pregnant she was too scared to tell anyone. 'I thought, no it'd go away – you know how thick people can be!' Looking back on all this four years later, Annette is able to remember how overwhelmed she felt but at the same time she can laugh about it. Although she shared some of Emma's feelings of awkwardness, she draws on her sense of humour:

> The Doctor turned round and said to me, 'Is there any chance of you being pregnant?' 'I'd rather not say.' I shall never forget that day. Then my Mum looked at me and the Doctor looked at me and I said, 'Oh yes there could be.' I felt so hot, I felt so embarrassed – 'Oh God, they know what I've been up to.' I mean, everybody does it, but not at 15! (Annette)

Most of the girls were aware that the news of their pregnancy would be a bombshell both at home and at school so that their own feelings about the pregnancy were dominated by their anticipation of the reactions of others. For Jane, pregnant at 14, now aged 23, her anticipation of those reactions led to her decision to keep the pregnancy a secret:

> I just knew I was pregnant. Then when my period didn't come ... We had been taking precautions but not on this occasion. That's how I knew ... I was very scared to tell anyone. Very scared ... I just couldn't bring myself to tell anyone. Not cos of the shame, it was just ... It's unbelievable that Mum and Dad never noticed at all. Not the teachers at school. No-one said a word. I block it all out now. I forget that I had ... I know I was young but I forget that it was such a secret. It's really weird.

Jane decided immediately to keep the baby. This was in spite of the fact that she too was not, as she put it, maternal:

> I never liked children. I used to hate babies. I would never pick them up. We never had any in our family ... But obviously your own children are different.

Although concealed pregnancies are often seen as pathological, Jane was very clear that she had not denied the pregnancy to herself. She obtained books on pregnancy. She felt the baby kick and was aware of it growing. She also planned ahead by saving money from a Saturday job so that she could buy things for the baby after it was born and the secret was out.

Francine became pregnant at 14 and could not bring herself to tell her parents until she was six months pregnant. During this time she coped by putting it out of her mind:

> I didn't think there was a baby inside me. I just tried to put it out of my mind. I knew I was pregnant but I didn't think there was a human body, a human person inside me. I just kept myself as if there was nothing in there. I just tried to completely cut it out of my mind.

Francine believed even the baby was aware of the tension, of the need for secrecy:

My Mum says he's very close to me. He seems to sense my mood. He only started moving when everybody knew and I was relaxed. It was as if 'I'm not allowed to move'. Then he began to move and kick and he was there.

Out of this difficult time, Francine finds it possible to extract a positive meaning. She sees the baby's behaviour as indicative that he is aware of her feelings and this view is reinforced by her mother.

Only one of the mothers, Nancy, expressed the idea that she was pleased to be pregnant even though she hadn't planned to get pregnant:

In the back of my mind we knew that if we carried on, eventually I would get pregnant but you just push it to one side. 'Oh, I'll deal with it when it happens.' You don't realise how serious it is until it does happen.

Nancy had asked her mother if she could go on the pill but she had refused:

She was dead against it. She said it was like saying I could just go out and have sex. That was it. She just didn't want to know, which was a complete surprise to me because she'd always been very, not lenient, but always talked to me about difficult things, you know.

When Nancy realised she was pregnant, she had concerns about telling her mother:

I felt happy but I felt scared as well. That was just the scared part of having to tell people. My Mum and Darren's Mum and Dad. But I think that because we were so young, we were happy about it but we felt we shouldn't have been – because we were so young that it shouldn't have happened. I suppose right from the beginning I did feel, 'Oh, I've got a baby and from now on I'm going to be called Mum and I'm going to be a Mum.' After that I always felt happy about it.

Nancy was unusual in making the connection very early on between the fact of pregnancy and the idea of being a mother, and it seems to have been this that confirmed her feelings of happiness at being pregnant. Unlike other young women who connected getting pregnant with embarrassment about their sexual relationship or anger with themselves for not using contraception, Nancy immediately thought of being a Mum and saw that as a source of satisfaction. Far from seeing herself as having a spoiled identity, Nancy anticipated motherhood as giving her a positive identity.

Only one of those interviewed had seriously considered abortion. Kim had been in trouble with the police when she was younger and had been received into care. She had been in a children's home and ran away; and then she was in a foster home and ran away from there. She ended up back at home. She had been excluded from school for a year and had only just started at a new school when at the age of 14 she found she was pregnant:

I didn't want to get pregnant. I went down the hospital to get an abortion. They said come back next day but I didn't go.

Kim could not explain how she had made that decision. She told how she wanted to be sure that as she was going to keep the baby, the baby should be healthy:

I give up smoking during the pregnancy. I didn't drink, I didn't smoke. I started up again after I'd had her but not while I was pregnant.

Such a decision suggests that Kim too had a sense of the developing child inside her and perhaps that sense of the reality of the baby led to her decision not to have an abortion. As with several others, Kim did not consider herself well suited to motherhood and others shared this view. 'I didn't think I'd have children. No one could see me as a Mum.' However, the rebellious and determined spirit which led to her running away from placements in care stood her in good stead in enabling her to cope with the fact of her pregnancy. The decision to keep the baby was not as clear as it was for many of the young women, but it led to a sense of commitment to the welfare of the child.

It seems that the reactions to the pregnancy might be seen as going through a process from fear and shock to fatalistic acceptance. Even when the pregnancy cut across what the young women had previously anticipated as being their plans for the future, they reached a point of accepting and learning to live with the pregnancy.

Family reactions

For all the young women, the first thought when the pregnancy was discovered was 'How can I tell my parents?' All were scared about the prospect and some put it off for several months as a result. The reactions of parents had an impact on how girls coped with the pregnancy.

It is possible to draw out several types of experiences which girls had in relation to their mothers. For some, although there had been initial fear of the mother's reaction, the announcement came in the context of a warm and close relationship. Wendy described her mother as:

Giving me all the options. Have an abortion, have it adopted, or keep it ... She accepted it. She said, 'I'll do whatever I can to help' and she did.

This pattern of response seemed to be the most useful by communicating that there was a choice to be made, not attempting to influence that choice, and offering uncritical support whatever choice was made.

Although the message, 'You make up your mind and I'll support you in what you decide' was a position stated at some stage by a number of the mothers, the message received by the girl was not always that straightforward.

65

Francine, for example, had put off telling her mother for several months until a friend told a teacher and the teacher encouraged her to tell her parents:

> My Mum was just upset, totally flabbergasted, upset. My Dad was just upset. My brother, I was very close to my brother and my Dad blamed him for introducing me to Patrick and he wanted to go and smash Patrick's face in. He was so very upset. Everybody was. It was more upset than anger. Everybody just cried really. They couldn't believe it ... The reason my Mum was upset was because I'm the baby and she thought, 'Oh no, the baby's growing up after all.'

Even three years on, the family's distress came over very strongly. Francine's parents had been ambitious for their children, her older brother had become an accountant. Francine was 14 years old and six months pregnant so it was too late for an abortion. Francine's first response to her family's questioning was that she would have the baby adopted. This was accepted by all parties including the boyfriend's parents, as being the right decision. From the way Francine describes the situation, she seems to have been overwhelmed by the feeling of sadness and responded with this offer of an outcome which would restore 'the baby' of the family to her former self. However, she changed her mind:

> Up until the month before the baby was born I was going to have him adopted ... It was when the social worker came round and asked me to sign the papers, I said 'I can't go through with it. I want the baby.' They'd even started to vet a couple but I said 'I'm very sorry but I want to keep the baby.' My Dad said 'I'm too old to have a baby in the house again.' My Mum wanted what I wanted.

Certainly Francine's parents by their reaction initially encouraged her to turn away from the option of becoming a mother, but she made what was then a very difficult decision to keep the baby.

For some young mothers the fact of the pregnancy was accepted by their own mothers but because of concern as to how the father would react, it remained a secret between them for a while:

> I was amazed. I knew that I was pregnant at two months but we didn't tell my Dad till I was four because my Dad would have had the pregnancy terminated ... My Mum and Dad have very different attitudes. He was absolutely terrible about it. He went over the top. He got in the car and drove off. Just to calm down a bit, just the thought of me being pregnant. (Christine)

Christine and her mother were very close and, in fact, Christine had been taking the minipill with her mother's consent at the time she conceived. The fact that the pregnancy was 'women's business' was reinforced by the different reactions of Christine's brothers and sister:

Both my brothers wouldn't talk to me until he was born. They didn't say a word. My sister stood by me all the way. She had a daughter when she was 21 and she was unmarried so she knew how I felt.

That different reaction between mothers and fathers was particularly dramatic in Barbara's case. She was the oldest of four children and at the time her parents had separated, when she was about 8 years old, she had told the Court welfare officer that she wanted to live with her father. She and all three younger children remained with him. This had worked well until he married again and tensions developed with her stepmother and her father over her boyfriend:

We got engaged. My Dad wanted to know if I was pregnant because I hadn't come on. My step-mum used to keep all my dates down in her diary without me knowing. So she was invading my privacy.

When the pregnancy was confirmed, Barbara didn't know what to do:

I was confused and scared. Then my Dad said I'd have to get rid of it. He said he was going to kick me out if I didn't get rid of it. So I made an appointment to have an abortion. Then my Mum said I could go and live with her if I was to keep it.

Barbara's father's reaction was quite extreme but seems even more excessive given that Barbara herself was born when her mother was fifteen years old. This fact might explain why her mother was willing to forget old differences and offer Barbara a home.

For some mothers, the closeness with their own mothers was rather overwhelming because their mothers greeted news of the pregnancy with delight and were keen to look after the baby themselves. This attitude led to an assumption that the young woman was going to keep the baby and that assumption was in itself irksome. This is how Nancy described her situation:

My Mum had said 'Oh, keep the baby even if you feel you can't actually look after it, I'll bring it up and later on if you feel you want to take over and look after it, you can have it' ... and Darren's Mum said, 'Oh you'll obviously keep it' but his Dad actually sat down and said, 'This is what's going to happen if you keep the baby or have you thought of an abortion, this will happen. Have you thought of adoption' ... He went through it all but they ... his Mum thought he was horrible suggesting that I should get rid of Peter but ... I would say he was the best one because he did put it all to me.

It seems to have been important to Nancy that she was able not only to make the choice but for the choice of keeping the baby to be seen as positive. At a very fundamental level, that experience of being offered a choice and being treated as a responsible person who can make such a choice for herself, is the first step towards seeing herself as adult. It is interesting that for Nancy this was not someone who was close to her emotionally. Perhaps that degree of distance was helpful.

Some of the young women's mothers were negative about the baby and the pregnancy, although these were a small minority. Kim's mother had wanted her to have an abortion and so told her to leave when she decided to keep the baby. Kim then relied on her boyfriend's family to give her somewhere to stay.

Emma's mother's attitude was more complex. Emma was set to be a high achiever at school and her mother was also working hard and going on a variety of professional training courses:

> She knew there was something wrong but at first she said 'I'm glad it isn't drugs or shoplifting' ... because she thought you could solve pregnancy. She thought I'd have an abortion, she thought *that* was the solution. I had to decide that weekend and when I'd decided, she wouldn't talk to me for a month or so. She decorated the bathroom and she'd sort of lock herself in the bathroom. Then when I started getting bigger and it got to one or two months before I had Sarah, she started to show more interest, like helping me think about what to get.

It is impossible to know exactly what was going on in Emma's mother's mind, but clearly the effort of coming to terms with her daughter's pregnancy cost her a great deal. Emma's stepfather was able to be more distanced and was the one who gave Emma the options in a more enabling way – although even for him the issues weren't simple:

> His sister can't have children so he didn't want me to have an abortion, which was really nice of him because he said if I wanted to, he'd understand but he doesn't want me to but if I really wanted to I could and he wouldn't say anything.

The complex feelings which Emma struggles almost incoherently to describe are characteristic of the feelings that family members expressed. Emma was grateful that her stepfather was giving her the message that he would support her whatever her decision but clearly that message was complicated by what she knew to be his own feelings about abortion. The way in which the stepfather's views are influenced by circumstances involving his sister is also a reminder of the way in which all participants in this family drama draw on a whole range of feelings deriving from their own family of origin, their own experiences as a child, etc. The presence of a pregnant girl – at 14, even a pregnant child – inevitably stirs up profound feelings in all concerned.

As the pregnancy progressed most young women drew on the care they received within their own families. There was potential for conflict in this but also potential for growth and a sense that the family worked together. For Nancy, the pregnancy made her dependent on her mother so that she felt looked after like a child herself. This was clearly a very special feeling:

> I was sick a lot the first three or four months, but my Mum was really
> good. She did everything for me. Spoiled me. I think that was nice
> because you felt – I'm pregnant, I'm important, everybody wants to do
> everything for you ... She still felt that I was still little. She felt she had to
> look after me and the baby, which was nice I must admit.

There seemed no contradiction to Nancy in being pleased at the idea of
becoming a Mum, accepting that responsibility, and yet enjoying being cared
for by her mother. It seemed that like any adolescent for whom the mother's
task can be seen as giving the right kind of care to enable that child to be
independent, Nancy was comfortable during the pregnancy in accepting that
care.

Emma had enjoyed not specifically her mother's care but more the feeling
of being the centre of attention:

> That's the best bit, being pregnant. You get all that attention. That's why
> women get post-natal depression, because they get all the love and
> attention. Then as soon as the baby's born, everyone's 'Oh, the baby.'
> That's why they get depressed.

Looking back on the range of reactions within the family, it seems that the
overwhelming reaction among the parents was one of sadness caused by their
own sense of loss and the concern that their daughter would herself lose out
on her chances in life. Even those who reacted with anger, whether against the
girl herself or against the boyfriend, seemed to be mainly shocked, overwhelmed
and simply unable to know how to deal with the situation.

The girls in the centre of all these powerful emotions seemed to value those
parental figures who were able to put the choices to them in as balanced a way
as possible and then support the girl whatever she decided. Although a
mother's assumption that her daughter would keep the baby was seen as more
acceptable in this group than an assumption that the girl would have an
abortion, it seemed important to most to feel that they had made a proper
choice.

The baby's father

For some of the mothers the relationship with the father of the baby seems to
have been central in their ability to cope with the idea of the pregnancy but
they were in the minority. On the whole it seemed that even when the
relationship continued during the pregnancy the young women restricted the
level of involvement of the fathers.

Two of the fathers were no longer in a relationship with the mother when
the pregnancy was confirmed. None of the other fathers left the mother when
the pregnancy was confirmed and the relationships continued. It was difficult
to trace the impact of the pregnancy on the quality of those relationships. It

seemed that where the relationship was already close the pregnancy provided a focus of shared concerns. Where the relationships were more uncertain, the young women saw the pregnancy as their responsibility and the young men were marginalized.

Tracey who had already ended the relationship at the time of the pregnancy being confirmed, did not believe that the father had any rights. She seemed to want to keep him at a distance:

> I split up with the father. We split up before I found out. He knows but there's not much he can do. If his parents knew they'd throw him out. (Tracey, interviewed during pregnancy)

Sandra had told her boyfriend when she realised she was pregnant:

> He wasn't that bothered really. He was a bit worried till my Mum found out. He was more worried what people would say and that ... I don't think he really understood.

Sandra's boyfriend didn't really see the pregnancy as something that would affect his life and was not thinking of the ways in which it might affect hers. In fact, Sandra was still in a relationship with her boyfriend two years and another pregnancy later but he had continued to live with his own parents. Sandra seemed to have accepted that pregnancy and indeed motherhood were her responsibility.

Few of the young women seemed to believe that being pregnant would speed up the move towards marriage. Barbara (interviewed while pregnant) had got engaged but said:

> I don't want to get married till I'm at least 18. My boyfriend wants me to get married at 16 but I want to live with him first to see if I can put up with him 24 hours a day.

There was no sense that during the pregnancy there was a need to legitimise the situation and the child as soon as possible. In keeping with their age, most were more preoccupied with sustaining relationships with their families.

For the three for whom the relationship with the baby's father was important, their boyfriends' reactions to the news of the pregnancy was distinctly positive. Nancy had felt quite happy to be pregnant. She and her boyfriend seemed to see the pregnancy not as awkward and problematic but as something which enabled them to take on adult roles and have the pleasure of their own child:

> Once I'd got used to it, I mean, I'd always wanted to be a Mum ... That was nice. I think Darren liked it as well. Oh, I was pregnant, I was having his baby and he was to look after me, that's the way he felt ... As soon as he found out I was pregnant, he took over fatherhood. He grew up. He wanted to get involved. He wanted to help me pick maternity clothes but then my Mum stepped in and whisked me off to town and he was really upset and nobody could understand except for me. I felt that he was

really shut out and that I was the one who was pregnant. He was just, 'the bloke who got her pregnant'.

The struggle between Nancy's boyfriend and her mother caused her great distress. At this stage she appears to have given in to pressure from her mother but at a later stage after the baby was born, she was forced to choose between them and chose him.

Christine's boyfriend was also pleased she was pregnant, although she herself had mixed feelings:

I don't think there's any words you could explain how I felt about it. I felt bad in myself. When I did actually get to see my husband and told him that I was pregnant he was over the moon about it. He'd had a girlfriend previous to me. She'd had the pregnancy terminated so he was pleased.

In fact for Christine, closeness to her boyfriend was encouraged by her mother once the pregnancy was known about. Her mother invited her boyfriend to live with Christine during the pregnancy, which Christine liked. They did subsequently marry and had been together for nearly four years at the time of the interview.

Finally, Annette's boyfriend was relatively low key in his acceptance of the pregnancy, 'I've made the mistake as well as you. I'm going to stay' was his first reaction, but his commitment during the pregnancy impressed her:

He was only on a YTS scheme but she had everything new. She had a new pram. He saved up each week, and a new Moses basket. Every Friday he used to come up and it was pay day and he'd say 'I've brought the baby something.' Even if it was just a pair of socks, that meant a lot to me.

This support from him was particularly important because of some of the rejection Annette was experiencing at school, which I shall deal with in the next section. Annette's boyfriend was black and she had been subjected to racist abuse.

With these few exceptions, babies' fathers were rather shadowy figures. This does not appear to be necessarily in line with the stereotype of the teenage boyfriend who won't face up to his responsibilities. The picture that comes across is that boys can take on the responsibilities of parenthood but that this only becomes likely where the boy/girl relationship has some future. Young mothers did not generally feel under pressure to legitimize the child by marriage and most girls were more concerned to avoid a bad marriage.

School

For very young mothers, the fact of being at school when the pregnancy is confirmed involves the need to face up to some kind of disclosure in a particularly public arena. School is a place characterised in this context by two significant elements; first, the people who operate within the school are divided into two groups – the children and the adults. Adults are powerful people who control and take responsibility for children. Secondly, schools attempt to establish a basic moral code, i.e. there is considerable emphasis on good behaviour as opposed to bad behaviour. The pregnant school girl challenges both the distinction between adults and children and the nature of sexual morality.

When a girl is pregnant and at school, the very fact that she is about to undertake an adult role with adult responsibilities cuts across the traditional divide within the school between adults and children. How is a teacher going to address a class of children which includes one adult? It could be said that teachers of fifteen year olds today do not see them as 'children' but they still in effect control, direct and have responsibility for them. The pregnant school girl can represent a challenge to that model of pupil/teacher relationship.

When a girl is known to be pregnant at school, she brings with her into the school situation an area of morality which in the main schools have no say in and, apart from some sex education, little influence over. The young offender who shoplifts and is on a supervision order is not necessarily identifiable within the school and therefore to a degree leaves his moral problems at home. In contrast the pregnant school girl cannot help but announce to the world that she has had sex, has not used effective contraception and is keeping the baby. All three are open to value judgements.

The young mothers in this study described a range of responses by school to the news of their pregnancy. The most extreme cases occurred where girls described being threatened with exclusion from school as a result of the pregnancy. Two girls mentioned this experience but the attitude of the school was rather different in each case. Wendy described the reaction of the Deputy Head:

> I said 'I'm pregnant'. She said, 'What are you going to do?' Their immediate reaction was that I'd either have an abortion or have the child adopted, even though I'd have been leaving in the May, three months later. I said 'No, I'm going to keep it.' They were quite shocked. I was in 'O' level exam groups. They decided it was not right. They said 'If you decide to carry on with this pregnancy, we'll have to expel you. You would be a bad influence on the rest of the school.' So I said 'I'm leaving anyway.'

Wendy saw the situation as very much a power struggle to ensure she conformed to their view of what was 'right':

> The school bent over backwards to help a girl who was having her baby adopted because she did what *they* wanted her to do.

What was striking here was the apparent absence of discussion around the issue of what outcome would be best for Wendy and what her views were

72

about that. The atmosphere is more like a debate about Wendy not wearing school uniform, i.e. a sense in which the school has the right to comment on behaviour even in such a complex personal area. From Wendy's point of view, this kind of attitude appears to have hardened her resolve to make her own decisions.

Christine's experience was also of rejection at school. When told of the pregnancy her head teacher said, 'You have been a total disgrace to the school, getting pregnant.' In this single sentence there is a whole series of messages. First there is the idea that Christine's behaviour in her private life is not only of interest to the school but reflects on the honour or reputation of the school. Secondly, there is the message that it is 'getting pregnant' that is the disgrace. Is this because it is immoral to have sex or because it is foolish not to use effective contraception? There is also the possibility that she may have done it deliberately and that her decision to become pregnant is the disgrace. There is a message of total lack of concern for the welfare of the girl herself. It is the welfare of the school that is the issue. Finally, the tone has its own message. It seems likely that the role of head-teacher or perhaps simply the role of adult, enables her to air her prejudices without regard for the feelings of the child in front of her.

Wendy and Christine both recounted these experiences with great emotion. They were still indignant and angry years after the event and what came across was their sense of humiliation. Having struggled with their own reactions to the pregnancy, having coped with the difficult business of telling parents, they then had to face the school. Fortunately both girls were well supported by their families which enabled them to feel sustained in their self-esteem. A different reaction at school would have helped although the determination of both girls to do things 'their way' was hardened by the hostility.

Annette's experience of informing the school of her pregnancy was affected by the fact that she had hated school and truanted as much as she could:

> They assumed I'd done it because I hated school and that it was the easy way out which that hadn't even entered my head because I still had to go down Robert Milne (the tuition unit) so I hadn't got out of it. Mr Johnson, who's the best teacher at that school, he was brilliant, he was good to me when I didn't want to go to school, he said 'I understand how you feel, Annette.' When I found out I was pregnant, I said 'Everyone's thinking it's deliberate, just to get out of school, but it's not', I said, 'I was ignorant as well as all the other people what get pregnant. You just never think it's going to happen to you.' He said, 'I know that', he said, 'but you do get the occasional teacher who says we know why she got pregnant' ... which it does look, now I see it, it does look like I done it just to get out of school. I mean it wasn't. I'd rather have stayed at school ... not that I regret having Kirsty but I'd rather have stayed at school than got pregnant at that early age.

73

The struggle for Annette to assert her own view of events was hard. In the face of a consensus of rumour and gossip about herself, there was no way of putting the record straight. The role of the sympathetic teacher, who accepted her version on trust was significant for Annette in sustaining her in the face of criticism.

More common among the pregnant girls' experience of school, was the concern by the staff that they would be a bad influence. Emma was told it was better to transfer to the tuition unit because her boyfriend was at the school and 'they didn't want me to influence the younger children.' Tania had had a good response from staff initially:

> It was just a nice school. Most of the staff were very nice as well and when I fell pregnant my teacher was really good to me and my head of year were all good. I would have been happy to stay at school ... but they wouldn't have liked me being there pregnant, encouraging other girls.

Rejection at school was also experienced by some as a result of the attitudes of the peer group. Where the peer group was critical this was resented by the young mothers because of the hypocrisy involved. The three who remember rejection by peers most vividly were also the three to whom school staff had been antagonistic. Christine recalled:

> I got called some very unpleasant names. I realised I didn't have any friends. I got expelled from school. When I left I was literally called a slut. They said I didn't know who the father was, which I did. I was just the unlucky one.

Christine described an atmosphere of sexual rivalry among the girls at school:

> Everyone had to go to bed with everyone else's boyfriend ... I don't know how many girls I know who've had abortions and I just don't agree with it.

Christine wanted to establish her own moral high ground by her opposition to abortion.

Annette also described a peer group culture where sexual activity was common but attitudes were confusing and contradictory:

> We was down the alleyway cos we all used to have a fag like you do at school and my friend come up and whispered, 'I had sex last night' and I said 'You never!' and I was so shocked. She thought it was great, fantastic. Then my other friends used to come up and tell me the same thing. Then when I fell pregnant, everywhere I went 'We know what she's been up to'. Then 'She's gonna have a nigger for a child'. I wasn't bigheaded about it, knowing I'd had sex – all I felt was totally embarrassed to think I was so young.

In this situation, although Annette picked up on the hypocrisy to a degree, she herself felt embarrassed about having had sex and being pregnant, so the comments about that reinforced her own view. What she found more difficult were the racist remarks about her baby and the strong support of her boyfriend was therefore critical because in that area she did feel isolated and vulnerable.

Wendy was more robust in her attitude to her peer group. She had become pregnant the first time she had sex and she was unmoved by comments made:

> Half the people who were saying things to me had been at it a long time before I had, they just hadn't got pregnant. You see, I think it might have been a case of all of a sudden, this person, whether they like it or not, if they're pregnant they're the centre of attention. Some people can't handle that. Back, deep in the back of their minds.

Wendy's notion that envy is a factor in the reactions of her peer group has interesting implications. Given that all girls are brought up to a greater or lesser extent with the idea that their destiny and future fulfilment lies in their role as a mother, then the decision either not to have sexual relationships or to use contraception has to be a rational act geared to postponing that role until all the circumstances are right, i.e. preferably married, with a house and having experienced the world of work. When a girl becomes pregnant, as Wendy did at 15, and decides to keep the baby, it is as if she challenges that idea and suggests that motherhood is achievable in the absence of those things. What is more, it is as if she hasn't deserved the attention she now gets because she hasn't worked, saved, found herself a man and postponed the satisfaction of motherhood. She is getting attention even though she is morally and culturally deviant. Such ideas seem helpful not only in explaining the reactions of other girls but perhaps also the rage of the adults.

Envy, however, is likely to be only part of the picture. What emerges from peer group reactions is that sexual activity is acceptable as long as it is largely secret and preferably separated from the possibility of pregnancy and motherhood. It is this latter point which some of the mothers seem to suggest when they talk of their attitude to contraception, i.e. 'I just thought it would never happen to me.' The separation of sex for pleasure from sex for reproduction is so much part of our culture, that we do not give it a second thought. The pregnant school girl, however, reminds her peer group that there is a connection and this threatens their sense of security in their own sexual relationships. This is perhaps another factor in the apparently hypocritical criticism of the pregnant girl.

It may be that such attitudes have started to change. Certainly the two girls most recently pregnant did not meet negative reactions from their friends or the staff. Barbara reported a generally positive experience of reactions at school and was the only one to comment on the reactions of boys to the pregnancy:

The school were pretty good about it. People have made me clothes and given me cards and presents ... A few of the boys said something nasty but that's boys for you. All the boys come up to me and want to put their hands on my stomach and feel it kick. Pretty good really.

Barbara was someone who felt more comfortable than most with the idea of her pregnancy, (She was interviewed during pregnancy and after the baby was born) and this enabled her to discuss any unkind comments lightly and to take pleasure in the idea of the boys wanting to feel her baby kick.

Most of the girls remained only a short time at school following the announcement that they were pregnant. This was generally because by the time the girl had realised she was pregnant, had it confirmed, told her parents and then told the school she was several months into the pregnancy. Although this was the case, feelings certainly ran high for those girls who were treated badly by the school. For Wendy this had happened eight years ago but she could describe it as if it were yesterday. It is yet another reminder that the pregnancy of a young girl is an inherently stressful time and that at key points in the process of coming to terms with it, such as going public with the news at school, long-lasting feelings of resentment can arise.

The tuition unit

As described earlier, the tuition unit at Robert Milne Family Centre became the education resource offered to all pregnant school girls in Ipswich soon after it was set up in 1982. It replaced home tuition and was seen by the schools and the education authority as preferable to the girl remaining at school. Few of the girls had any memory of how the decision to move to the tuition unit was made or on what basis it was decided when in the pregnancy it would be best to transfer. Most could remember that an education welfare officer was involved. Tania said that she had wanted to stay at school but that the education welfare officer had decided she had to go to the unit. Barbara, in contrast remembered seeing the education welfare officer and herself asking to start at the unit early in pregnancy because she felt tired. On the whole the girls seemed to assume that they would come to the unit and transferred when they were told there was a place for them. Although there was a preliminary meeting between the girl, her mother and the unit teacher, the girls were not sure what to expect from the tuition unit.

The staff

For most of the girls what they found was a safe haven in which their pregnancy was not seen as something to be ashamed of:

At Robert Milne they treated you as if you were grown up. They didn't make you feel like a child who'd got into trouble. They still helped you with your work and just carried on. If I was pregnant and still at school, they'd have thought, Oh, she's pregnant, that's going to disturb her work. Steve (the unit teacher) made it seem like it was an extra bonus ... She made you feel that just because you were having a baby doesn't mean you can't go to college, have a job, do what you want, which was nice. (Nancy)

Nancy sums up a number of themes here which were each taken up in different ways by other girls. First, the fact that girls felt treated like grown ups and not children was frequently mentioned and seemed particularly special. Francine echoed Nancy's words:

It was nice really. Steve sort of treated you as an adult, not a child. We were learning still but she didn't treat us as if we were kids ... Steve prepared us for accepting our responsibilities. Teachers tend to look down on you. You're only a teenager – you don't know nothing.

Francine was not alone in drawing the comparison with teachers at school. As she phrases it, the criticism seems to be not only of the way a teacher treats pregnant girls at school but the way teachers treat all young people.

Although it seemed important to be treated as an adult, i.e. acknowledging the difference that the pregnancy made, it also seemed important that things should carry on as normal. As Nancy pointed out (see above), a school might expect less of you because you were pregnant. In the tuition unit the message was it was possible to keep on learning and be ambitious for yourself:

Steve felt sorry for people who couldn't be bothered ... She'd do anything for them, to know they would be doing something when they left school. (Emma)

In this context the unit was able to encourage some girls to achieve more than they had at school. Kim, who had never attended school regularly and had been out of school for a year, enjoyed attending the unit. Christine had also missed a good deal of school and attributed her examination success to the unit. Even those who had been doing well at school felt they had benefited:

I was there from February to May. I learned more in those three months than I did in the last three years at school. (Wendy)

Although most girls attended only two days a week the expectation was that work would carry on at home:

If she don't think you've done enough on one subject she'd tell you. If you hadn't done the homework properly she'd get on you to do it again. I never had that problem because I liked working. At home I got on with my work. (Christine)

So the key elements so far seemed to be being treated as responsible adults not wayward children and being treated as normally as possible in terms of school work. The teacher appeared to have hung on to the value of education for the girls and far from lowering her expectations she gave them the impression that if they were to become responsible mothers, they would need to make use of all the educational opportunities they might get.

Although the academic work was seen as important by the girls, the need to be supported and accepted was at least as valuable:

> I don't know how Steve does it. She's great. We were all different but she never ever made any judgements on anybody. There to give help and advice if you needed her. Never said You're right or you're wrong. She just backed you all the way. And when you're that age you need some backing, whether you're right or you're wrong ... Support's the most important thing at that time. You can always catch up on your education later. (Wendy)

The informality of the unit seemed important. For many, the idea of being able to have a cup of coffee when you fancied one was the sort of touch which helped them feel relaxed and cared for.

The close attention of the teacher was not universally enjoyed. Tracey found that being on her own with the teacher, it was difficult to just get on with work herself:

> You get so much help it seems as if they're doing it for you. I've often thought why don't I hand it over and let her do it?

Jane found the expectation that she would want to discuss her feelings with the teacher to be intrusive:

> I would never talk to her but then I am not that person. I work things out for myself. She wanted to know what was going on in your life. She wouldn't wait for you to say.

Clearly there is a balance to be achieved and it cannot be assumed that all pregnant school girls have the same needs educationally or emotionally.

The group

Just as it was a relief for most girls to find themselves treated as adults and offered a comfortable balance of education and support, so most also found the company of other girls in a similar position very reassuring:

> It was nice because you didn't have to not talk about certain things. I felt that I was a bad influence on all the other girls at school because I was the one who was pregnant. Not that anybody said anything. I hadn't done anything wrong. I'm just the unlucky one who got caught. You could talk more openly and that and discuss what you were going to do when the baby was born. You had more in common. (Nancy)

Nancy is here linking two problems that have been identified previously. The feeling, which she herself had, that she was a bad influence is linked with that sense of moral bad luck, i.e. she wasn't any more immoral than others who have sex but she was more unlucky. The difficulty of asserting this rather complex position is overcome in a group of people in a similar position, who know exactly the pattern of events which can lead to an early pregnancy. Christine makes a similar point:

> We could all sit there and talk. We know what we were talking about whereas if I'd spoken to anyone from school they wouldn't have known what the hell I was on about.

The fact that each group of girls shared the experience of being pregnant did not mean that they necessarily had other things in common. For some, the small groups at the unit brought them into close contact with girls who normally they would not have chosen to spend time with. This became in itself a learning experience:

> I didn't know what to make of everyone at first. Some of the girls looked so hard but when I started, I started with two of the hardest girls there. They both stood at the gate and waited for me and I've got on really well with them since ... I wouldn't have got on well with those kind of girls at school but we're really good *friends*. We stop and talk for about an hour. (Christine)

On occasion, the numbers attending the unit fell, sometimes because several girls were at home with babies and did not attend again until the baby was six weeks old. When this happened it was possible for a pregnant girl to be attending on her own. Where this had happened, the absence of the group feeling was commented on, although rather ambivalently. Tracey said that she was on her own in the unit class. 'It would be better with other people – nice to have someone to talk to but we'd sit at separate tables so there's not much difference.'

Barbara said that it 'got a bit boring' when she was on her own but added, 'Coming on my own I get more attention and get on with the work. I do more work on my own.'

Barbara and Tracey talked less about the emotional impact of the unit and saw it very much as an education provision which enabled them to attend part-time and helped them complete their work. It is perhaps relevant that these two girls had not experienced criticism at school and were still attending some lessons there. Both felt fairly comfortable with the idea of being pregnant and were not looking for reassurance from the group, although it is possible that if they had had more experience of a group this would still have been of benefit.

79

During the interviews, all the young women were asked whether they felt the unit was able to offer a sufficiently broad education. As is described above, the climate generated by the teacher was such as to encourage achievement and most felt they had worked hard. However, there was a range of opinion as to the viability of such a small unit in meeting their needs for subject choice. In this particular area, there have been some changes over the years that the unit has been operational.

In the early days of the project, there were difficulties in persuading schools even to co-operate in supplying books or information as to the examination syllabus for each subject. Wendy remembers having to find out who would accept her for exams and said this depended on the subject teacher's attitude to the pregnancy. All of the girls studied mathematics and English and often child care but the range of other subjects that they could take was limited by the amount of time that they attended the unit, i.e. two days, the resources of the unit, and the particular skills of the teacher. For some this wasn't a problem, generally because they had missed out on some of their basic education and the unit gave them the opportunity to catch up. Others were disappointed. Tania would have liked the opportunity to stay at school and was critical of the education received at the unit:

> The teacher wasn't qualified to do the subjects such as computer studies and social studies. I had to do child care. I was never doing it at school. I gave it up to do metalwork and woodwork. I had to do a whole course on it in a matter of weeks.

Tania was also critical of the fact that she had such a short time in the unit to do the work. She also attended at a time when there was no creche, so babies were around in the room where the girls were trying to work.

Although Tania had valid practical reasons for her dissatisfaction with the unit, it seemed that for her the main problem was that she had enjoyed school and felt resentful of the need to move to the unit. Her family had been quite accepting of the pregnancy, so she was not looking to the unit for the kind of emotional support which others valued.

In recent years the curriculum in the unit has become more flexible as individual packages are worked out for each girl. The girls interviewed who were present in the unit at the time of the study had not in fact made a complete break with their school. Barbara had wanted to continue with science and so during the pregnancy had returned to school for certain lessons to finish the required course work. In addition, when it was realised that she could be entered for a French examination, a home tutor was allocated to give some individual tuition. Similarly Tracey was returning to school to take graphic design classes.

This flexibility seemed to affect not just the range of subjects taken but the sense in which these two girls did not feel as heavily reliant on the unit as a source of support and identity as mentioned above. They seemed to move easily between the tuition unit and their previous school.

The antenatal classes

An important part of what was offered to girls by the unit during the pregnancy was antenatal classes. Although they were prepared to go to the hospital for medical checks and although they saw themselves as in many ways like older mothers, they expressed the feeling that they would not have attended antenatal classes alongside older women. On the whole they felt that they'd had a helpful series of sessions, not just on the birth itself but on other issues:

> It helped a lot. I hadn't a clue about anything. We saw people about contraceptives, the health visitor, the midwife – really good, ever so good. I learned so much while I was there – just to get those kinds of skills, first-aid, etc. (Emma)

Others commented on the fact that there had been some straight talking as to whether labour was painful. On the whole the evidence that seems to matter is that the girls described their labour in a way that suggests they felt well informed about the process.

The medical profession

During the interviews, few young women singled out doctors for special mention in connection with pregnancy. Prior to the pregnancy one or two had approached their general practitioner to ask if they could go on the pill. The response to that request varied widely. One doctor had seen the then fourteen year old with her mother and prescribed the pill, albeit the minipill which she subsequently suspected had proved inadequate as a form of contraception. Another doctor when faced with a similar request from Barbara, also aged fourteen, said that if she had been nearly sixteen he would have agreed. He also told her not to have sex because 'that could ruin your insides'. Barbara then tried elsewhere:

> I went down the family planning clinic but they said I must have a parent with me because I was under 16. I spoke to my Mum about it and she said she'd take me down there and put me on the pill but my Dad said he'd sue the doctor if I went on the pill. So we never bothered.

The only girl to report a particular experience at the hands of a hospital doctor during pregnancy was Wendy. When she had her first antenatal appointment at the hospital she saw an obstetrician. When she told him she had decided to keep the baby, his reaction was critical:

81

'You can't. What happens when you want to go out to clubs and pubs?', It was very upsetting. I'd made my decision. By the time he was finished with me he'd more or less said I was useless, I was going to live on social security for the rest of my life and that it was disgusting that I should be bringing babies into the world. But that wasn't helpful at all. I'd made my decision and he was there to look after me antenatal wise not any other way. I don't think he understood that you've got to judge each case on its own merits not on what you see before you. He thought I was going to have the baby, when it was three months old, run off and leave it, which was exactly what he said to my Mum. My Mum knew I wouldn't just desert a child.

Wendy, articulate as ever, conveys strongly the power of that attack on her integrity. The doctor was clearly incensed by the sight of this fifteen year old who was so confident in her decision to keep the baby. Not unlike Wendy's head teacher, he feels able to indulge his prejudices and be rude and offensive to his patient. The power of his position, the power of being an adult and perhaps the power of being a man enable him to denigrate her. Fortunately for Wendy, she was supported by her mother's confidence in her. In reflecting on this experience she is able to analyse the doctor's problem, i.e. he shouldn't judge on what he sees before him, his only responsibility is for her antenatal care and so on. However, Wendy's feelings ran very high in describing this scene. Even brief experiences of criticism and rejection , or indeed help and support, retain their significance when they occur at a time of such vulnerability, as discussed earlier.

According to these young mothers, the unit seemed to have been the focus of education, support and preparation for the birth of the baby. The positive impact of the unit seems to have far outweighed what might be imagined for a resource which was only attended for a few hours a week over a period of several months before the birth. This says a great deal for the quality of the service provided for such a potentially vulnerable group.

11 Birth

Giving birth alone

In some cases, the nature of the pregnancy determined the nature of the birth experience. For Jane, who had concealed her pregnancy, this was most striking. She had gone to school as usual that day but had returned home when she went into labour and told her mother that she was in labour. They went to the hospital together. Although Jane had read books about childbirth she had not been to classes or discussed it with anyone. She was barely fifteen years old. In spite of the fact that she was frightened, the hospital decided that her mother should not be allowed to stay with her during the birth:

> It really was weird. It really was horrible. I didn't have a clue. But they didn't want my Mum in just in case there was something wrong with the baby. Also, because of the circumstances, that I wouldn't keep her. They wanted to take her out without anyone seeing her.

The idea seems to have been that because Jane had not had antenatal checks and scans there was an increased likelihood of the baby being abnormal. Further, that even if the baby were normal, the fact of it going for adoption made it undesirable that the grandmother should see the child. It seems incomprehensible that a young girl should go through childbirth unaccompanied by a family member or friend when the services for adult women are so totally geared up for partners or friends being present. It is as if the unusual circumstances led staff to abandon a rational, let alone a sensitive, response to her needs and she was left on the receiving end of an extremely punitive decision.

In the event, the labour went smoothly but after her daughter was born, the staff wanted to take her away because they had assumed she would be placed for adoption:

They didn't ask me. They asked my Mum who said it was up to me. I said 'No' to adoption. She said 'I've got to see what Dad says but if he says OK keep the baby then no problems.' I'd decided already but my Mum was asked before me.

Jane, in fact, did hold her baby:

It really was nice. Lovely. It was just brilliant to have her and to have it out in the open. It was such a relief.

After keeping her tremendous secret for so long, the potentially fraught pregnancy had ended in a new grandchild for her parents. As Jane had anticipated, there was little said to her afterwards and she was able to enjoy her baby.

Although Jane's circumstances were unusual, she was not the only young mother who had to face the labour alone. For Nancy too, it was, according to the hospital, the risk of a problematic birth which led to them excluding her boyfriend:

Because Peter was breech birth they wouldn't let him in. Maybe if I'd asked they'd have let my Mum in but I didn't want her there. I wanted Darren and that was it.

In fact, Nancy had spent the latter part of her pregnancy trying to establish her relationship with Darren and his rights as a father as her priority in the face of a mother who found it hard to let her go. It is remarkable that she felt so determined about this that she gave birth alone rather than appear to have given in to her mother.

Nancy and Darren both distrusted the hospital's reasons for excluding him and it is something that she became very distressed and angry about when describing it:

I still say to this day it was because he was not my husband. I don't know ... the midwife and nurses said 'We can't see why you can't go in' but the doctor said Darren couldn't come in, which was horrible because he was out there and being so young I was terrified of what was going to happen. It wasn't as bad as everybody says but I wanted him there for support. He wanted to come in so much and for him not to come in was horrible ... He felt he didn't have any *right* because he wasn't my husband.

That sense of powerlessness in the face of the system had clearly lived with this couple subsequently. Whether the unconscious motive of the doctor was punitive towards Nancy or Darren as individuals or whether he took one look at Darren, a seventeen year old boy, and concluded he had no place in a delivery room is impossible to know. What is clear though is that far from making extra efforts to ensure that a very young mother had the support of the baby's father if she wished it, she was denied a right which would have been extended to any older woman, married or not.

One of the mothers was on her own because her mother and boyfriend had been sent away when the labour was apparently not progressing. Christine had a baby that was born with a serious abnormality:

> I was in labour twenty-four hours, had an epidural and then had an abnormal baby with bowel and intestines on the outside of his body. The staff had never experienced anything like it. I was so drugged up I didn't know what was going on ... The baby was born at 4.22 and was at Great Ormond Street by 6.30. I gave birth but had no baby. It was terrible.

Christine had had a very relaxed pregnancy. Her boyfriend had moved in with her and her mother was very supportive. However, the traumatic nature of the birth left her in shock. Her boyfriend and her parents rushed to the hospital and her boyfriend was able to hold the baby briefly before the baby was taken to Great Ormond Street. This had been important to Christine, who had been told that the baby might not survive. The joint support of her boyfriend and her parents at such a time helped Christine cope with the stress of the birth.

Grandmother present

The presence of the mother's mother could result from a whole range of circumstances. This section will describe the circumstances surrounding the presence of a number of mothers and consider specifically the young woman's feelings about that and the impact it had on her experience of the birth.

Kelly and Tania both came from households full of women, both being one of four daughters in their families and having no brothers. Kelly was pregnant at the same time as one of her older sisters and she talked about 'going through the pregnancy together.' She had wanted her Mum to be present:

> My Mum was there the whole time, the labour, the delivery ... I wanted Mum not Scott (her boyfriend). It was a plain sailing birth.

Although Kelly had had an easy birth, as she saw it, and her mother was present supporting her and they were both pleased with the baby, this did not prevent a midwife mentioning the possibility of adoption:

> Someone suggested adoption after I gave birth to him. I thought 'Of all the bad timing!' I felt like getting up and thumping her. But for the fact that I'd just gave birth, I'd have got up and hit her. That's just me and my temper. I said to her 'You stupid cow.'

Again the hospital staff fell back on prejudices and assumptions and failed to consider the feelings of the young woman who has just become a mother. Kelly's response was characteristic of the fifteen year old she was fiery, determined and talking the language of the playground. However it was also a positive, spirited and entirely appropriate response in defence of her new identity as a new mother, a rejection of the assumption that she would be giving up the baby because of her age. It was clear from the whole interview that Kelly found her mother's support very necessary but on this occasion it is Kelly's temperament which makes her round on the unsuspecting midwife.

Tania also chose to have her mother with her at the birth rather than her boyfriend:

> It was like shelling peas. I went to sleep and they had to wake me up to give birth. It was a lovely simple birth. There's my Mum going 'Scream Tania' 'No, I'm fine thank you Mum.' I had my sister there as well ... My boyfriend went to the pub. He came round but I said 'Just go out, leave me alone.' I didn't hold her the first night because I had a drip in my arm. All I wanted was a cup of tea and a Mars bar. I was so hungry. And my Mum and sister were walking her about.

There is a strong sense in this account of birth as being 'women's work' and it's not surprising that the boyfriend was excluded. In fact, Tania said she cared a great deal for her boyfriend and had hoped to marry him but the birth experience she wanted to share with the women in her family.

Wendy had not had a close relationship with the father of her baby and for her it was obvious that her mother would be present. However, unlike Kelly and Tania, Wendy had a difficult birth:

> I've got a bit of a problem. I get pregnant really easily but I can't get the baby out again! They induced me and I was in labour for forty hours after the inducements but I didn't dilate and so then I had a Caesarean section which was fine and then I got an infection so I had to go back into hospital. If I hadn't had my Mum I wouldn't have been able to cope. I was so ill I couldn't even feed the poor little boy.

For Wendy, the difficult labour, the birth and the subsequent infection had become a blur in her memory and her mother's role in being with her and looking after her child was what enabled her to cope. Wendy's mother had been extremely positive and helpful during the pregnancy too, attending antenatal appointments and so on. Her mother's role at the time of the birth seems to have occurred comfortably as a natural extension of a close mother-daughter relationship.

The young mother herself may not be sure who she would like to attend the birth. Francine seems to have felt unsure about what she wanted, as she had during the pregnancy. Having planned to have the baby adopted until the month before the baby was born, she had asserted herself in changing her mind and upsetting her boyfriend's parents. When it came to the birth she was again aware of the strong views of other people and seemed at a loss:

> Patrick (the baby's father) wanted to be in on the birth but my parents didn't think it was right. Because I was too young to be pregnant, I was

too young to have sex and I was too young for that. I sort of wanted him to be in on the birth but I didn't know really.

Perhaps these parents' attitude sheds some light on the hospital's role in isolating young mothers in previous examples. There seem to be two elements to this, firstly being too young to have sex and too young to be pregnant, she was possibly seen as too young to receive consideration as an adult at the time of the birth. A second possibility is that the birth itself is seen as an intimate, almost sexual experience. For two fifteen year olds to share that experience may seem like a further challenge to notions of decency. Finally, for Francine's parents, it was also a way in which they reasserted their role as carers for their dependent child.

From Francine's point of view, she simply accepted what had been decided. Her mother was present and Francine describes a very normal birth. In fact, she is not unusual in describing even a long labour as something she was able to get through quite easily. Francine had been in hospital for twenty four hours in slow labour:

> By 3.00 they really started taking notice. I was walking around. In the end they had to burst my waters at about half past six and they gave me gas and air. That was no good so I told them, 'I'll just do it straight.' The birth wasn't too bad. I had Mark at 7.34 ... I had quite a good birth.

From these four brief examples it seems that where there has been a close relationship between the mother and her mother through the pregnancy and the baby is to be welcomed by the mother's family, then the presence at the birth seemed a natural and supportive part of the experience. In Francine's situation, she had put off telling her mother for six months, then chosen adoption for two months, finally deciding to keep the child. She had received a variety of messages from family members about this decision and at the time of the birth was still only beginning to anticipate taking up the role of mother. She did not seem able to describe having any feelings about her mother's presence.

Birth with the boyfriend present

A minority of the study group had the baby's father present at the birth although a further two would have liked this to happen if either the hospital had allowed it or the labour had been more predictable.

Kim had had a difficult pregnancy, having had bad indigestion and persistent vomiting. Her labour was also one of the difficult ones:

> I was there for about eight hours. They started me off. The inside water busted but the outside never so they busted the outside. They gave me an epidural and they cut me from back to front and they give me forceps and I lost a lot of blood.

Kim neither grumbles nor complains about this experience and what 'they' did to her. She did remark that it didn't hurt at the time but it certainly did afterwards. Her boyfriend had been with her and her Mum had been in the waiting room 'all that time'. For Kim, the significant aspect of the birth had been the health of the baby. She told me the baby weighed 8 lb. 6 oz. and was healthy because she had made a point of giving up alcohol and cigarettes during her pregnancy. In this sense the baby herself rewards Kim for all her efforts. The boyfriend was mentioned only in passing but this was characteristic of Kim's attitude to him. He seemed a marginal figure generally and it was rather unexpected that he should be there at the birth. Her father had told her boyfriend that if Kim was to keep the baby, he must take care of her, so perhaps this was the first step.

Annette had been supported throughout the pregnancy by her boyfriend, Michael:

> My Mum was there as well but she was in the waiting room. I didn't want her there. From the start he said 'I'm going to be there when you have the baby' and I said 'fine that's up to you.'

She described the labour as 'long but very straightforward' and she was able to walk around:

> There was a lovely sister on there and she was the one who explained everything, and she was the one who delivered her and she was absolutely brilliant. I couldn't ask for anyone better. She talked me through the whole lot. I mean she couldn't explain it properly because every birth is different.

This touch of wisdom at the end was part of Annette's philosophy and was shared by other girls. It was helpful to have plenty of help and advice but 'every birth is different.'

> Once I'd given birth I really did enjoy it. That was the best time of my life. Michael was there with me. I'll never forget it. 'I just can't believe it!' he said.

Annette and Michael had a very positive experience of the birth of their child. Annette was able to choose who to have with her and who not and had the help she needed from hospital staff.

Barbara was interviewed a few weeks after her baby was born. She was 15 years old and gave a bouncy account of her experience of childbirth. Barbara's waters broke in a garage so she called her boyfriend and went to the hospital:

> They said I was contracting but I couldn't feel it. They gave me a drip to speed it up but about 8 o'clock I wanted a painkiller. They gave me an epidural but at quarter to 12 I was only dilated 3 centimetres so they gave me an epidural Caesarean ... My boyfriend was there. I could see everything they were doing reflected in a light fitting. I could see them

cut me open and the womb come out with the baby in it. At first going up to theatre I was worried about seeing it but I just watched it and it was really good. I could feel them pulling the baby out. It was an amazing feeling – when they pulled the baby out my tummy went flat. It felt really good.

I had thought when I interviewed Barbara during the pregnancy that she seemed rather resilient but this account of her birth was quite extraordinary. Not only was Barbara herself coping well, her boyfriend was laughing and called out during the operation 'I can see them pulling you apart. I can see your intestines!' The idea of these two teenagers taking such an experience so very much in their stride was impressive. What was also impressive was that it was expected by hospital staff that if the father was around even though he was only young, he would be at the birth. Perhaps obstetric practice has moved on since Jane and Nancy were denied the possibility of having someone with them because the birth might prove problematic. Barbara and her boyfriend are good examples of what is possible. Many older men and women would find an epidural Caesarean quite a test. Perhaps because hospital staff were matter of fact about the boyfriend's presence, this enabled them to relax and be themselves.

What came through all the description of the births was the essentially normal range of emotions expressed – the fear, the joy, the powerlessness in the face of occasional obstetric prejudice and the gratitude and appreciation when staff were kind and supportive, all seemed reminiscent of older mothers. The young women themselves appeared at times to be more in control of their feelings about the situation than the hospital staff. Hospital staff sometimes appeared to find it difficult to take their cue from the young mothers themselves rather than from their own anxieties about their age. The antenatal classes at the tuition unit had prepared these girls to handle the labour and the birth positively. They would mostly have had the opportunity to talk with other young mothers about the experience. Some were clearly more anxious than others and it seems that doctors and midwives will need to approach each young woman with an open mind in order to establish their individual needs.

12 Motherhood

This section draws on a wide range of interview material. The young women reflected on the events since the birth of their child, recalled feelings and often generated their own theories for why things turned out the way they did. It is this ability to reflect on their own feelings and behaviour and the feelings and behaviour of boyfriends and families, which makes the material so illuminating. In the centre of it all is the newcomer; the baby whom I had seen as a recipient of mothering, became through the mother's accounts a key actor. All the women had widely differing experiences but the one thing they had in common was the sense that this child was a special child and that if this had not been the case, they could not have coped. This is a theme to be described in more detail later.

Before embarking on the young women's individual experiences it may be useful to begin by describing in broad terms the practical phases that a young mother in Ipswich would go through. The first phase, after discharge from hospital, was generally spent in the mother's own family home. Two of the mothers moved fairly soon to their boyfriend's family home but in essence the principle was the same. The mother was still dependent on parents and was able to look to them for advice and support in addition to food and a roof over their heads.

The second phase has varied over the years. When the mother felt that she wanted or needed to live independently she was likely to have to persuade her parents, usually her mother, to write a formal letter evicting her. Once categorised as homeless, she would go to a homeless families unit or bed and breakfast accommodation. If after a period of time she could show that she was able to pay rent reliably, she would be given council accommodation. In Ipswich this was generally a 2/3 bedroom house with a garden, although some mothers were given flats. The period of time in the homeless families unit was a minimum of about five months. It is possible to spend 18 months there but none of this group was in temporary accommodation for more than a year. On occasion, mothers have been able to show that their family home was overcrowded and have moved straight into a house or a flat. The point at which each mother decided to leave home and start out on this process varied greatly.

The mother's personal resources

All of the women drew on different accounts of support but for some they had the sense that they had survived because they were 'strong' people. In order to examine that idea, it was necessary to look at the kind of attitudes that these women had to becoming a mother and the way in which they believed their own inner strength had helped them cope.

Having concealed her pregnancy, it is perhaps not surprising that Jane was equally selective about the amount of support/influence she would be prepared to accept in mothering her daughter, Ruth. Ruth had been born in Jane's penultimate year at school so Jane returned to school in the September leaving Ruth with her mother during the day:

> I went back to school but it didn't work out. My Mum and Dad wanted the baby for themselves which is a little bit understandable ... We really had clashes. Mum wanted to take over and I wouldn't let her. So in the end I had to go, which was definitely the best thing.

Jane went to the Council who told her she'd need a letter of eviction:

> So I gave Mum the pen and paper to write the letter. I've never got on with my Mum not now, not then. So I went to the homeless families unit.

When asked whether at just turned sixteen, she felt she was still young to cope with this, she replied:

> Oh yes, but I knew I could cope. You know, you *know*. I definitely knew I could cope. Some people can't you know.

When as a 'sensitive' researcher I made sympathetic noises about being a sixteen year old with a five month old baby in a homeless families unit, Jane soon put me straight:

> It was brilliant. Also it's like I had my own money as well. I was there five months. You pay weekly this little charge of £10. If you keep that up, they think you're a good candidate, you get a house. At sixteen it was brilliant. There was all these people in the same situation. You get together and you have a laugh. I mean, the homeless families unit is like the last straw but to me it was like an open gate to getting a house.

For Jane the experience of being independent was important but she also enjoyed being with others in the same situation. For Jane that meant, homeless

91

women and children, *not* young mothers. She was happy to join the world of adult women and managed without the support of her family.

Although Jane rejects to some extent the idea that age is relevant to coping, she had been clear about what she could and could not handle and planned her life accordingly. When given a house, she had a boyfriend:

> We never lived together. He lived at home and I lived at the house, which suited me fine because I didn't, you know, want that. I was too young to have that. It would have been too much for me to have someone else living with me.

Jane distinguishes between being old enough to be a mother and being old enough to have a live-in boyfriend. She attributes this to the fact that she just needed to spend time with her child:

> It was just at that age, it just wasn't tiresome at all. Like I said, she was a good baby. I was just doing things with her. I just wanted it to be me and her ... Nothing was difficult but you grow up with them a little bit.

In this discussion Jane draws on her ability to trust her own feelings. She made her choices without, it seems, reference to other people's ideas of what is expected and is very matter of fact. Since that time her experiences seem to have confirmed for her the sense she had that being pregnant at a young age was not necessarily all bad for her.

Sometimes the fact of adversity led to mothers feeling an even stronger drive to succeed. On these occasions, difficulty at the birth came to be seen as part of a whole range of challenges which the mother had to overcome. Wendy had to have a Caesarean delivery and had been very ill afterwards. Her baby boy had also been ill and admitted to hospital. She hadn't thought of herself as maternal before but had to adapt:

> Yeah, I found it quite easy in the end. It's the bonding there. With him being ill and me being ill and so many people against me saying Oh you've got to have an abortion, that's not right, I just dug me heels in and I was stubborn. I thought, 'Right, I'll show you!'.

The word 'stubborn' occurred in several interviews. Whether naturally extrovert like Wendy, or quiet and determined like Sandra, the mothers felt that their stubbornness was an asset. It seemed an interesting choice of word. 'Stubborn' is a term parents often apply to children to describe the fact that they won't give way to the views of those older people who know what's best for children. Hudson and Ineichen (1991) refer to this stubbornness as a problem because it means young mothers won't take advice. Wendy's use of the word suggests more of a fighting spirit, which can be of benefit in the context of very early motherhood, given the stigma and other pressures which they experience.

Annette drew her self-esteem in the early days as a mother from her sense that she had what she saw as an innate ability to look after her baby:

92

I was in hospital for 7 days. They wanted to keep me in because obviously my age, I was young, plus it was my first child, but I *knew* what to do. I knew how to make a bottle up. I mean they came round because they always do ... I said I know how to do that and they went away and came back and said, 'Sister thinks we ought to teach you because you're very young'. I said 'I can do it' and I done it but I'd never done it before ... I took to it like a duck to water, it just came to me.

Although there had been this very promising beginning, when Annette went home she began to suffer badly from postnatal depression:

I was a totally different person. I used to be happy-go-lucky but I'd totally changed. I'd lost so much weight. All my energy and my interest went into her. Everything in my life consisted of her. No time for Michael. No time for my Mum. You feed, you change, then you put them down and then it's time to do it again.

Annette's depression went on for nine or ten months during which she continued to live at her mother's home and attended Robert Milne Family Centre, doing voluntary work. She also saw a psychiatrist. At the end of the day, though, she felt that she had forced herself to break out of her depression:

I looked at her one day in her Moses basket and thought 'You poor little child, look what a mother you've got.' After that, I thought 'That's it! I'm not going to take my tablets any more. I am going to manage' and I did.

Although Annette acknowledged how helpful people had been, she seemed to recall this moment in time fairly specifically as a point when she felt that her feeling for the child, her feeling as a mother, had enabled her to gain strength enough to overcome the depression.

This kind of raised self-esteem was put to the test by subsequent events. Annette became pregnant again soon after this and was so ill during the pregnancy that she spent four months in hospital. After her son Adam was born, she and her husband and the children were rehoused in a flat:

We were a happy family, a girl and a boy. I was so pleased with myself. I couldn't wish for a better time. He was a good little boy. She was helpful. We thought this was our year.

Sadly, at the age of three months, Adam died of a cot death. Although in some considerable distress, Annette took charge of the situation and it was she who wrote to the Council:

I said 'I know I'm supposed to be in the flat a year but I'd be most grateful if you'd find me somewhere else to live because my son died of a cot death and I'm finding it depressing and hurtful living here.' They gave me this house.

93

Annette was still only eighteen years old and had to care for her two year old daughter and her distressed husband. When asked how she coped, she replied:

> I got myself together. I thought although it seems awful, life has to go on. He'd been ill from day one and everyone who came to see me said he'd got an angel face. He didn't look like a girl and he didn't look like a boy. I thought it was meant to be.

Throughout the interview with Annette, she regularly found ways of explaining her world which drew on ideas of fate: the idea that she knew how to make up a baby's bottle without having done it before; the idea that one day, she looked into the Moses basket, decided to manage and her postnatal depression disappeared. Here the idea that Adam had an 'angel face', that he was too good for this world and that his death was 'meant to be' enabled her to cope. Annette concluded the discussion by saying 'I'm a coper, a survivor. The more things I've coped with, the easier it is to cope with something.'

Although Jane and Annette had to draw on personal strengths to cope with particular circumstances, all the young mothers had to negotiate with families and boyfriends as to what level of control they were to have over the upbringing of their child. Although most were happy about some level of help and advice there was a general feeling that, rather like Annette, mothers – even young mothers – could be relied upon to know what was best for their child.

Sandra was a very shy and rather self-effacing young woman – very different from the more outspoken members of the study group. When asked whether being in the homeless families unit was a difficult time for her and her baby, she replied 'No not really. For some people that would be. Otherwise that weren't, not really.' When asked if looking after her daughter, Susie, was how she imagined it would be she replied:

> I don't know really. I suppose everybody's different. I don't know how I'd have looked after her if I'd have been older or anything. I just looked after her the way I thought I'd look after her. I just brought her up how I thought was the best way to bring her up. I mean I had people telling me what to do but it used to go in one ear and out the other. I just let her do what ... things in her own time.

In contrast to what is often suggested about young mothers, Sandra was relaxed about her child's progress and comfortable with the idea that the child would dictate the pace. When I asked her whether she always felt as clear as this:

> Sometimes I am and sometimes I ain't. I just go on as the day goes along. I just tend to go day by day as the day goes on.

In fact, Sandra had a great deal of support from the family centre and was very appreciative of that. Her attitude may come from the reassurance she has received there, too. She perceives herself as the right person to make decisions for the child because she is the child's mother but is able to accept help.

Not all the young women who had to fall back on their own resources did this by choice. Tania, one of four daughters, had found her family to be supportive during the pregnancy and labour but after the birth she found herself isolated:

> Mum said when I was pregnant, 'If you decide to keep the baby Tania, I'll help you out. I'll baby-sit and you'll still have a bit of time to yourself.' But when it actually came down to it, no she wouldn't baby-sit. So I was stuck in constantly. My boyfriend felt he was too young to be a father anyway and we sort of drifted apart because we never had any time together.

The difficulty in sustaining a relationship with the baby's father while living with her own family caused problems to a number of mothers. For several it was what prompted the girl to move into a homeless families unit. In Tania's case, her boyfriend ended the relationship.

Tania also felt bitter that she was isolated from her friends:

> They all said they'd come and visit but I never saw any of them. I never saw anybody.

When Tania did decide she wanted to move out, her mother refused to write a letter so that she could be formally classed as homeless. There were occasions when rows between Tania and her mother occurred and Tania did get into the homeless families unit. However, when an official from the housing department visited her mother, she would agree to have her back. Tania felt quite powerless:

> I'd be in the homeless families unit and because she said she'd have me back I had to go back. We kept moving in and out and my little one kept getting upset with moving backwards and forwards.

Although Tania found being a mother harder work than she had thought, 'I couldn't believe how much work was involved once I had one' and although she experienced a great deal of pressure in her relationship with her mother, she felt confident that she had cared for the baby quite well:

> I didn't really have any ideas – it just sort of came naturally. You learn by your mistakes, I suppose.

She remembered being reassured by a health visitor at the baby clinic:

> She said 'Kerry's always clean, she's well cared for'. That really used to make me pleased. 'She looks really well cared for. I know you look after her and she's lovely.'

Such comments raised Tania's self-esteem and sustained her in the face of difficulties at home. Looking back on the early years of her daughter's life, she feels reassured that in spite of conflicts she was a good mother but she has some regrets:

> I wish I'd enjoyed her more at the time. I think I was too young at the time to really enjoy her. I feel I've missed out on a lot.

The role of the child

When the first mother interviewed described her child as really rather exceptional, it seemed that this was a way of making quite a strong statement about herself as a mother. There was the sense that the child she had made was a good thing and there was the sense that in caring for this special child she had become rather a special mother.

The same idea was then expressed in various ways by all the mothers. Perhaps their sense of the child as being special was a particularly significant part of these young mothers' experience. Jane was the most clear on this subject. Although she attributed much of her success as a young mother to her basic strength of character and determination, she also believed that the baby contributed to her coping. Her account of events was punctuated by references back to the baby:

> She was a very good baby, lovely child, always has been. Brilliant ... I have no trouble with her, she's just a brilliant child. Mick (her husband) says it's a shame she's not his but with saying that she wouldn't be who she is now. Not one regret at all. Brilliant child. I would go through it all again basically because then I'd get the same little girl I've got now.

Although Jane's daughter was the product of a relationship which was never serious, her temperament is apparently better than it would have been if derived from Jane and her present husband. What is more, all the difficulties were worth it because whatever the combination of circumstances, this child is someone to be proud of. Clearly as a message to give the child, it must raise the child's self-esteem and create a very favourable cycle of mutual affirmation between mother and daughter.

Wendy's description of her son was equally approving:

> He's a really, really smashing little boy. I know everyone goes on about their own kid but he's polite and mild mannered. He's a really nice little boy. He's great.

What was impressive was that even when describing a series of what might have been problems, she incorporates them into her very positive idea of him:

> He was always like that. He used to eat us out of house and home but it kept him quiet if he had food in his mouth. He had a bit of a problem with teething and that, but apart from that I've never had any problems at all.

96

He was a bit hyperactive when he was two but that was orange squash and when we cut that out he was alright.

At some fundamental level she believes in him. Each mother emphasised different aspects of the child that made them special. It could be both temperament and intelligence:

He was a lovely little kid. Everybody loved him ... He's so brainy. I don't know where he gets his brains from at all. (Kelly)

Often there was simply the sense that the baby or child was very forward:

He's very intelligent for his age. He talks ever so well for his age. (Francine)

She's going to be brainy, I reckon. Some of the things she does at home is what some of the kids are doing here (at the family centre) and she's the youngest one here. (Sandra)

For Kim, it was her baby's ability to gain weight that made her feel proud. She had been pleased that giving up smoking and drinking in pregnancy had lead to an 8 lb. 6 oz. baby. She had breastfed the baby – which was perhaps unexpected given Kim's stormy history of being in care, being excluded from school etc. Now that Chelsea was a toddler she was rewarding Kim by continuing to thrive. Kim brought a large studio portrait to show me how lovely she was.

In these examples the interplay between the achievement of the child, the pleasure which that gives the mother and the way in which that sustains the mother in her job of caring for the child is important. As mentioned in the previous section that sense of determination and stubbornness, that wish to 'show them' and succeed against the odds needs some sense of success to sustain it over time. That evidence is the child.

The role of the family

Because most of the mothers spent a period of time living with the baby within their own family, the first stage of the negotiation of a new identity as a mother was conducted in the same environment in which they had been a dependent child. There were extremes of acceptance and rejection, unconditional support and a degree of hostility. For all the women there was a very complex process going on in which the young woman and her mother, often a grandmother for the first time, and other family members had to negotiate new roles. Not surprisingly, strong feelings were evoked in other family members also by the presence of the new born baby.

What was most difficult for the young mothers in relating to their own mothers was to get the balance right between accepting help and advice and feeling that the baby was being taken over. There are two obvious parallels.

97

First, issues about control and the shifting balance of power between teenagers and their parents is a feature of most families. Secondly, for new mothers of all ages there are often tensions between themselves and their own mothers brought about by the reawakening of many feelings to do with their own mother/daughter relationship. For these young mothers these two potential areas of tension come together around the fact of the new baby's unplanned presence in the family home, the dependent child of a dependent child.

For some, establishing the comfortable level of dependence and the comfortable level of distance from the grandmother was relatively unproblematic. Wendy had her mother's support after the birth. Then with the passage of time the house became overcrowded, she was getting 'itchy feet' and obtained a house for herself from the Council which was just down the road. Now, at 24, she is pregnant again and her mother is around to help out in her business. The roles of mother and grandmother give pleasure to both.

On occasions the relationship between mother and grandmother are not particularly close or affectionate but the grandmother has still played an important role at a particular time. Annette's description of her mother was, 'A lot of people don't get on with my Mum. I mean, I don't but I've got to thank her for letting me stay there.'

Annette, her boyfriend and her baby stayed at her mother's home, living in one room, until they got a house. During her second pregnancy she spent months in hospital and her mother looked after her daughter. In fact, she looked to her mother for practical help of this kind but used one of her mother's friends as a confidante. It seemed that in this way she established the degree of distance which she needed and was able to make choices about that.

Even Jane, who had left home with her baby and gone to the homeless families unit at the age of 16, said that she had learned a lot from her mother about how to look after a baby in the early months:

> Mum taught me a lot. How to look after her. I wouldn't have known how clean to keep her. There was some people in the (tuition) unit who used to keep them in the same nappy, the same clothes, but whether it was their fault, they didn't know what to do ... whereas I had Mum at the beginning.

Jane, in a sense, took what she needed from her mother. She learned but she kept in control and sought her independence when her mother's involvement with the baby became overwhelming.

When other grandmothers had seemed to take over the child, this at times appeared to be a result of their own emotional needs and at times was a result of circumstances such as the young mother's return to school. The young mothers were very unsure how they felt about it. Tracey, who was interviewed both during the pregnancy and afterwards was aware at an early stage of her mother's likely reaction to the baby. Her mother had been pleased about the pregnancy and offered to adopt the baby if Tracey felt she couldn't cope. After the birth, Tracey did leave the baby with her mother while attending the tuition unit and was planning to do a further college course. Tracey was worried that her son Jack would see his grandmother as his mother. The deal appeared to be that the grandmother would be caring for the baby so that Tracey could do more with her life:

> If I don't continue with a career, she'll never speak to me again because I'd be wasting my life. She left school at 14.

Because schools and colleges don't have free nurseries, Tracey knew that if she wanted to pursue a career as she had hoped she would need to stay in her mother's home.

Initially after the birth, Kelly went back to school and left her baby with her mother. However, she became depressed and left school. When she started to attend the tuition unit and wanted to take the baby with her, her mother reacted:

> My Mum wouldn't let David out of her sight. He was her first grandchild and first boy. He was mega spoiled.

Although Kelly did gradually assert her independence and got a house of her own, because she worked full time and her mother cared for the baby, there seems to have been a legacy of some uncertainty for her:

> David loves my Mum, he love my Mum. He'd rather be with my Mum than with us. She practically brought him up. She was there with his first steps, there for his first word – I was at work. It upset me, it really upset me a lot when if he fell over he'd say 'Nan' instead of 'Mum'. I used to say he's my kid not yours, leave him alone.

Kelly was very ambivalent about the role her parents played. She described their role positively at times:

> They've really been ever so supportive in whatever I've done. They're really good parents. I think they're the best.

Yet she felt that although they enabled her to work, go out at night and so on, she was not as close to her son as she would have liked. In fact, this was an unusual family in that the parents and all four daughters lived within walking distance of each other and Kelly, her son and husband were part of a very close extended family of aunts, uncles and cousins. Kelly felt equally ambivalent about the extreme closeness of the family – two of her sisters 'popped in' during the interview time – and at that time felt it was difficult to have any privacy just to be with her husband and children.

Francine, like Kelly, had gone back to school leaving the baby with her mother. This decision had been made following a suggestion by the tuition unit that since she had a whole year left at school, she may do better academically if she returned to school. Francine herself remembers wanting to stay in the unit but accepting the advice she was given.

Although Francine was quite pleased with her school results, there were definite concerns about the impact that leaving the baby with her mother had on her confidence:

> My Mum got really close to him. She's closer to him than her other grandsons. Sometimes I get a bit jealous when he says I want my Nan, I want my Grandad. My Mum says he does it to wind me up.

At the time of her interview, Francine was living at home having just split up with her boyfriend, the baby's father. Somehow being back in her parents' home it was even harder to hang on to her identity as a mother. This was somewhat compounded by her mother's suggestion that she should go out more, meet a new boyfriend, rather as if she were 'just' a teenager:

> As my Mum said, 'You've had no life anyway, Francine, you deserve to.'

This was a difficult message to disentangle. Is the only 'life' of importance to be that of a teenager without responsibilities? Were all her attempts to sustain a relationship with her boyfriend, care for Mark, create a nice home, were they not really living? One can hear so much of the mother's own feelings about her daughter's 'lost youth' and perhaps her own. These two women struggle together to find some way through their dilemmas so that grandmother–grandson, mother–daughter, young mother–son relationships meet their individual needs.

Apart from general concerns that the grandmother was taking over the mother's role, there were also disputes about how the children should be brought up:

> My Mum thinks they should be allowed to get on with it until they have hurt themselves and learn by their mistakes. I believe that they should stop before they hurt themselves. (Tracey)

> My Mum was supportive but then again as time went on and I was getting older, we'd never argued before but as soon as she started telling me what to do I didn't like it. (Emma)

> I want somewhere of my own. You can't look after your babe the way you want to because there's too many people around. (Kim)

In several situations it seemed that this was an important stage in which the young mothers started to push seriously for independence both emotionally from their families and practically in terms of getting their own accommodation. Rows about the child and rows about moving out were sometimes complicated by the fact that the young mother was helping to look after her own mother's young child. Emma and Tracey both had arrangements whereby they would look after their mother's child:

> My Mum was supportive – but I used to do a lot for her as well. I'd take Adam to school and pick him up. Do the housework and cook the tea.

Emma's mother was retraining for a different career and Emma saw her as being in as much of an identity crisis as herself.

In Sandra's situation, there was almost a complete role reversal. It was Sandra who became tied down to looking after her mother's baby which was eight months older than her own daughter, Susie:

> My Mum went out to work and I had my little sister and Susie. Then she started to go out at night a lot more. In the end I just had to move out ... I just couldn't hack it. Me and my Mum were having arguments every minute of the day.

Sandra was in a difficult position. Her Mother had stuck by her during the pregnancy and allowed her to continue living at home and she felt powerless to prevent her mother dominating her. Her only option was to move out into the homeless families unit, which for her was preferable.

From this section emerges important material about the delicate balance that needs to be achieved if the young mother is going to feel helped and supported rather than criticised or her role as a mother usurped. Listening to these women talking it became clear that it was not easy to achieve this balance and that the desirable balance was different for each family. Although this was largely a family affair, the role of the tuition unit, school and the varying availability of housing affected the girls' ability to make choices about the level of their parents' involvement. The choice to take what they needed in terms of advice and support in the early days and then move on when they felt emotionally ready was not available if they had already committed themselves to returning to school or were not able to obtain housing. Sometimes the grandmother could control the point of separation simply by not writing a letter evicting her daughter. Where the time together went on beyond the time when the mother felt she should have moved on, there was a legacy of frustration, bad feeling and concerns that the tensions had affected the child.

However almost all the mothers had felt helped or supported by their mothers at some stage and at its best it confirmed a pre-existing close relationship or in one case brought together a mother and daughter who had not lived in together for six years.

The fathers

Although the fathers of the babies were often one or two years older than the mothers, they were still very young to be fathers. They weren't interviewed for this study, but the role they played was described in various ways by the young mothers and the issue of whether or not they would be seen as contributing to the care of the child or the mother's ability to care for the child was of interest.

The women's relationships with the fathers of their babies fell broadly into three groups; those who had separated from the father before the baby was born or soon after; those who had maintained a relationship with the father but had had problems in the past or doubts about the future; those who had remained with the father, had married, set up home together and felt secure.

The first group, whose relationship with the baby's father had not continued, tended to dismiss him as rather an irrelevance. Tania was angry because he had not wanted to maintain contact with his daughter but the others had chosen to maintain a distance between themselves and the fathers. This would perhaps not be surprising in terms of their own relationship with these young men but in fact they did not consider that their child might need to see the father at some stage in the future, or that they would have some role to play.

Kelly had separated from David's father soon after the birth:

> We split up the month after David was born. He insulted me on the way back from the christening. He don't see David.

Kelly met another man soon after this and that relationship has lasted. David is now eight years old:

> I haven't told David about his real Dad. David thinks John is his Dad. I will tell him eventually.

Other mothers were more prepared to tell the child that there was a Dad who was no longer around but not who he was. Emma's daughter has never seen her father and knows nothing about him, but Emma doesn't think this is a problem:

> Apart from once she got upset because a child was saying when we went on holiday, you haven't got a Dad, but I just tell her she's special or whatever.

It was difficult to understand exactly why these mothers minimised the role of the fathers or whether this was in any way characteristic of the age group. There were few expressions of anger apart from Tania whose boyfriend had proceeded to marry the next girlfriend who became pregnant. There was no confirmation of the stereotype of the young man who deserts his girlfriend once the pregnancy was announced. Even Tania's boyfriend was still around when the child was two. However, given that in society as a whole such a large percentage of children lose contact with their fathers following divorce, we should simply see these young mothers as part of a more general trend.

Within the second group, there was a range of experiences of the baby's father but all had some problems or experienced some conflict between themselves and the father of the baby.

Kim and Barbara were both unwilling to make too much of a commitment and did not want marriage yet if at all. Kim had lived at various times with her boyfriend's family but found him to be very little help with the baby:

If he's in a room with her, he doesn't keep an eye on her. He'll watch television and ignore her. Wish he'd do more.

She hardly mentioned him in describing how she was coping with motherhood, and in planning for what she wanted by way of future housing, she intended to have the house in her name. They had split up 'loads of times' and she wanted to be in control of the accommodation and of her child.

Barbara was more positive about her relationship with the baby's father. She could imagine living together but she didn't want marriage yet. She had been affected when her parent's marriage split up, she said. In addition, she disagreed with the way he handled the baby. At the time of the interview she was living with her mother and her daughter was only six weeks old. Her mother had indicated that this would only be temporary so Barbara had to make a decision about the future. She wanted to live independently with her boyfriend and thought he should help her with the baby but she wanted to reserve the right to some control over the baby. During the interview Barbara shared much of her anger and distress about the way her father had rejected her when he married again and it seemed that although she was confident and coping with the baby, the relationship with the baby's father was a source of uncertainty and anxiety for the future.

Two of the young women were very preoccupied during the interview with their concerns about the relationship with the baby's father. Nancy's child was six at the time of the interview and she was married and living with the father. During the pregnancy a pattern had emerged in which Darren, her husband, and her mother had competed to be the person whom Nancy would turn to for support. Although she valued her mother's support she was inclined to feel that Darren was more important. By the time of the birth, as described earlier, Nancy made a stand on this issue, by refusing to allow her mother in when the hospital excluded Darren. Nancy went home for a few days with the baby but then moved in with her boyfriend's family:

> The first week was at Nan's with Mum. I wanted my Mum to be there but, my Mum, cos she was on her own and we were kinda like close, she thought she was the most important thing to me. She couldn't understand that I loved Darren and he was like the important thing. She wanted to keep me hers and not let me go. I kept trying to explain to her, whatever age, I'd have to move on anyway but because I was young ... if she'd have just let it go and let me get on but she said 'You've got to choose. If you go off with him, you don't ever come here.'

Nancy was in a difficult position. Having chosen to be with her boyfriend, he gave a similar ultimatum:

> Then Darren said, 'I don't want you to see your Mum.' For a while I never saw my Mum. I felt that we were like partners so I went along with him.

103

For a while it seemed that all was well. Darren, who had always been in trouble at school, did an apprenticeship and then went to college two nights a week. The relationship had not always been smooth. They got married when the child was two years old but had separated for two brief periods since. Nancy felt that these problems were related to their youth:

> He was going out every night. He had someone else. He was just catching up on his early years ... He had a friend who died and he thought 'I've got to 21 and I've done nothing with my life except for being a Dad'.

During one period of separation, Nancy herself, who had by now had a planned second baby, felt a taste of freedom:

> Nan said 'Go out a couple of times a week.' She'd baby-sit. I felt that I could relax and be 21. That was all those years going out as a couple. The first time I went out and felt 21 and I didn't have to worry about the children.

At the time of the interview Nancy and Darren were together again but the future of the relationship was a concern to Nancy because of the effect these separations had on their son, Peter.

Francine, aged 18, and her boyfriend had separated three weeks prior to the interview for this study and was living back at her parents' home with her son Mark, aged 3. He was having a relationship with another woman. Francine's feelings of anger and abandonment were compounded by the fact that she had had her first sexual relationship with him:

> We met through Church. He's two years older than me but we were both very young. I was his first sexual partner as well so when I found out about this other girl it seemed really weird. We both lost our virginity together and have had nobody since.

The fact that she was a mother with responsibilities also meant that the competition was unfair:

> He's gone off me. I have been dowdy, been at home, got the baby, got a bit boring. She's out to work. She's out there, she can have nice clothes, a bit of make up ... So last week I went out, had my hair permed, bought some clothes. I thought, 'I must get myself sorted out, I must feel better in myself.'

In addition her concerns for Mark made her worried about any future relationship for herself:

> I've had Mark's Dad with me. I'm going to have to find someone else who isn't Mark's Dad. How's he going to treat Mark? He might accept me but will he accept Mark? He might beat him up and be horrible.

104

Although many of these feelings must be common to any woman left to care for her child on her own, the feelings do seem to be particularly keen because of the early pregnancy. At the age of 16, Francine had a one year old child, and was living with her boyfriend in their own home. She had compressed several stages into a short space of time. She had survived the difficult family reactions to her pregnancy and coped with a year in which she attended school during the day and cared for her child at night. Having made it into a relatively settled life, it now seemed to her that she was back in turmoil and uncertainty.

From this second group of mothers with problematic relationships with the fathers, there emerged very few references to the fathers actually helping with the care of the children or having a close relationship with the child. There seemed to be no expectation that the fathers would do a great deal with the children and therefore not much complaint when they didn't. Kim did think her boyfriend should do more but on the whole they did not describe the young men as being active as fathers.

However, the interviews with the two mothers who had married the fathers and had secure relationships, also did not reveal any particular expectation that fathers should be involved in child care. Christine had felt very supported by her then boyfriend, Daryl, soon after the birth of John, but Daryl had since taken to working extremely long days and at weekends. Christine had constant contact with the women of her family but saw very little of her husband.

Annette had talked warmly of the way her husband had shown commitment during the pregnancy, buying things for the baby. In describing the family she did not mention the father's particular interest or involvement with the child currently, although this may be because she took that for granted.

Perhaps what was helpful was the general sense of security that the secure relationship brought and this was helpful to the women in coping with the role of mother. In that sense Annette and Christine had more in common with Wendy, Kelly and Jane who had separated from the baby's father but were each in secure long-term relationships with men they had met subsequently.

Certainly where relationships were unsteady, the young mothers felt much more anxiety about how to make sure the children felt secure. They were anxious for themselves and for the children. In each case the young mothers had the children's needs very much in mind.

Motherhood and the tuition unit

The pattern of attendance at the tuition unit following the birth varied according to the age of the girl, the point in the school year when the baby was born and whether or not the girl chose to return to school. In addition, the introduction of the creche in 1987 meant that some of those interviewed attended at a time when the babies were in the teaching room while others had the advantage of the babies being cared for in a separate room.

As in the earlier section on the experience at the unit during pregnancy, it seemed useful to divide the comments into those broadly relating to the academic work in the unit and those relating to the element of support. The latter category will include not only those comments which related to experiences during their official time at the unit but also those which relate to an ongoing sense of connectedness with the unit and the family centre as a whole, a feeling which for some was still strong eight years later.

The feelings about the unit's influence after the birth of the baby were varied. The initial sense of relief that some of them felt during pregnancy when they first transferred to the unit from school was in the past. They had now taken on the role of mother and had rather different needs.

Education

Some of the young women were glad of the opportunity to get qualifications in spite of having a baby to feel responsible for. The existence of a unit with a creche enabled them to achieve academically:

> If I'd have gone back to school I don't think I'd have passed any exams at all. I wouldn't have been able to concentrate. Here I could concentrate, knowing that Susie was close by. (Sandra)

If course work had been completed during the pregnancy the time at the unit after the birth was spent preparing for exams.

Emma stayed on to study for 'A' levels. She found it difficult working alongside younger girls who were at a different stage emotionally and academically. She did not pass her 'A' level examination but her drive to succeed subsequently in the world of work and her current study towards further qualifications to advance her career certainly suggests a continuing commitment to education. She still feels that staying on at the unit was the right decision.

What was important at this stage was the encouragement in the unit for girls to consider going on to some form of occupation after school leaving age. This was mentioned earlier by girls during the pregnancy, but for those who attended as mothers there was a message from the teacher that it was important to be occupied, even if not academically:

> Even if they had this attitude that they weren't going to do anything after they'd had the baby, then she'd let them work at the centre or ask them to come into the centre to keep their minds busy so that they wouldn't end up like cabbages at home. Not just schooling, but trying to push them on. (Emma)

Generally the feelings expressed about attendance at the unit after the birth revolved around issues other than the academic work. Kelly, who had not attended the unit during the pregnancy, talked at great length and with great enthusiasm about the unit without ever mentioning the work:

> I loved every minute I was there. They didn't have all the facilities that they have now but Steve was brilliant – we got on really well, though she had her hands full with us lot.

Support took a range of forms. For Christine, advice about being a mother mattered. 'Trying to help me to learn to be a mother properly.' This was associated again with the fact that they were treated as adults and as individuals with different needs. When Christine's baby was born with serious problems, and was in hospital, she was allowed to return to the unit early:

> I couldn't sit at home with nothing to do but worry. Steve let me go back after two weeks. Everyone at the Robert Milne Centre was absolutely great about it.

When her son John was discharged from hospital after six weeks, Christine was advised to spend two weeks at home with him to 'get to know him properly.' This was important to Christine because she was anxious about handling him and was tempted to let her mother care for him. In the event, she soon gained confidence.

There were many examples of situations where the fact that the unit was within a family centre enabled the young mothers to be offered a range of support mechanisms. Annette had suffered quite badly from postnatal depression and used to worry constantly about her baby and keep checking on her. She was invited to do voluntary work at the centre which enabled her to have a break from caring for her baby who was in the creche but left her close enough to be able still to feel available to her.

Where mothers were in the homeless families unit, they would be encouraged to attend more than the requisite number of days. The teacher would often collect the mother and child.

After leaving the unit, the mothers have had the possibility of returning to an annual reunion. Not all mothers attend this but for those that do it is an important occasion. Some mothers have attended reunions for the last eight years. What is more, there is a sense that the unit and the centre continue to feel part of their lives. Several mothers who were pregnant for the second or third time when interviewed mentioned that they would ring the unit teacher to tell her when the baby was born. Sandra and Kim, both currently aged 17, described themselves as having gone to the centre at 15 and having never left. Others mentioned popping up to the family centre to see old friends on the staff. Nancy sums up those feelings:

You'd walk around the centre and go in where all the little children were and even now when I go up I talk to all the women there, they still remember. So we did get on well – like a big family really. I always go to every reunion. I really look forward to going. It's really nice just to see how they're getting on. It's nice to go up just to see the women. Just after I got married I went up and one of the other women was getting married and we were talking about different colours.

Those who expressed enthusiasm for a continuing involvement with the centre ranged from those who were troubled in their lives to those who were secure in their relationships. The place itself seemed to bring back good memories of being cared about and it could be relied on as a link to a special time in their lives.

There was only one note of dissent about the role of the family centre. Jane, one of the first girls to attend the unit, had felt labelled as 'a problem':

I didn't like it at all. They'd got some rough people there. There was us and cos it's like a problem place so then you'd got these mothers who needed help. I didn't know why they needed help ... Then you'd get all these handicapped children as well. All these people with problems. Obviously I must have been one of these people with problems. I was normal but I had my child early. I kept thinking 'Why am I here?'

Jane remembered having lunch with these different groups and feeling out of place. However, she did feel it was better to have a tuition unit rather than home tuition and she did think it was better to have the unit in a family centre than at school. She simply didn't know why a family centre implied problem families and she has been someone who has chosen not to continue the contact:

There's this yearly thing when they all get together. I've never gone to one. That's just not me. That's past.

On balance the unit was seen by most interviewees as a positive part of their experience of being mothers. It was seen as providing active help but also as reassuring by its continuing existence. Although the centre relates closely to the social services department, it is significant that those who were enthusiastic about the support they received were clear that they would not have wanted to see a social worker, except perhaps to have benefits explained. Kim had had previous experience of social workers:

I wouldn't see no social worker. I had them when I was younger. I hate them. I had a social worker checking up on me because I stole from my Mum.

Even those with slight knowledge of social workers were hostile to the idea:

I don't like social workers at all. They offered in the hospital but I've got friends who did talk to social workers and even now they still interfere so I just said no. (Christine)

Several of the mothers were also dismissive of health visitors, although they would take the baby to be weighed and checked at a clinic.

What emerges is that the unit at the family centre, by being associated initially and perhaps primarily with education is seen by most mothers as unthreatening. Therefore the advice, guidance and support which is offered as part of the antenatal classes and informally by unit and centre staff is seen as a combination of the sort of information a school might offer and the sort of advice concerned family members might give.

The unit therefore represents an important focus for gaining the trust of young mothers and enabling them to accept support and advice without feeling overwhelmed or threatened.

The role of work

Two factors suggest that work is an important issue to include as a distinct section. First, the literature suggests that it is in the world of work that young mothers suffer most from lost opportunities and the loss of sources of money and self-esteem which work can give. Secondly, although not all the young mothers worked, for those who did so, work was a very important part of their lives and they defined it as a way of not fitting the stereotype, i.e. young mother living on benefits.

The motivation to work could be quite strong:

I went to work when David was 7 weeks old. I don't know whether it was the thought of being out of work or if it was the thought of doing nothing but I couldn't bear the thought of living off social. I've never been one to ask for handouts – although it's not, you've worked for it, you're entitled to it but I'd rather sit and do a full day's work and know that I've earned the money. (Kelly)

Kelly's parents were able to look after her child and with the extended family around also, she felt happy with the arrangement. She had some feelings of resentment when David developed such a strong attachment to her parents but had no regrets about her decision to work.

Nancy also chose to work. She found employment when Peter was three months old and then went on a two year secretarial Youth Training Scheme:

My Nan looked after him. For a while my Mum took him. I felt that Peter went through a naughty stage and I did feel guilty but he was always with his Nanas.

Nancy also had hated the idea of living on state benefits and this only occurred during brief separations from her husband.

Wendy and Jane were two of the first young women at the tuition unit and were twenty-three years old when interviewed. They both had tremendous drive and had had varied work histories as they balanced their commitment to their children with their working life.

Wendy while still living at home with her mother started to work part-time as a waitress when Neil, her son, was a few months old. He was looked after by family members:

> It was just waitressing, ten till two, but it was worth it, just to get a break. Just a little bit so I can experience work.

When she got her own house, she gave this job up. She then turned her hand to dressmaking:

> I started up a little dressmaking business. I used to make clothes because I couldn't afford to buy them when I was at school, money being tight and all that and I got so many people saying will you make me this and that, that I ended up turning it into a little business.

The Council put a stop to the 'little business' since it was operating from a council house. When Neil started school, Wendy worked full time in a factory but she was too independent for this. 'I was so used to working my way, I couldn't work in a big factory, *their* way.' She left and took a beauty therapist job where she had some training:

> Then I thought – na, they're making too much money out of me. So I started looking for property and started my own business.

During this phase Neil was looked after by a friend who had gone to college and then had a baby. 'It just worked out great that one of my best friends needed the money when I had it to give her.' Having decided to set up a business, she found banks were unhelpful. 'They're very biased against you when they know you're a single parent.' So Wendy decided to buy her council house, get an additional £5,000 on the mortgage and used that to start the business:

> If you can't get it the normal way, you've got to go round the houses. It's not easy, but if you're stubborn enough and determined enough you can get there.

At the time of the interview, Wendy had a large mortgage, owned her own house, ran her own hairdressing and beauty therapy business and employed three or four staff. She still had plans:

> I'm going to build this place up and then I'll sell it and buy a little restaurant that I can live over.

Also at the time of the interview, Wendy was reaching the end of her second unplanned pregnancy:

> One of the worst times to get pregnant is when you're just setting up in business ... Contraception? Nothing's 100 per cent. If they're going to come they're going to come.

Wendy's history is given in some detail because more than anything else it suggests the way in which the early pregnancy was just one of the challenges which Wendy faced or in some cases set herself. Although this second pregnancy was also unplanned she was in a secure long term relationship and was planning to marry the father.

The meaning of work for Wendy went beyond the need to earn money. She wanted to do something with her life – not to impress anybody else or to prove a point but simply because she had the energy and knew she could do it.

Jane was not unlike Wendy in her level of drive but she had no support from her family once she left home and so whatever she achieved, it was very much on her own. Jane had moved to the homeless families unit at 16 and had been given a three bedroom council house when she was still 16. They had to make special arrangements because she could not formally be a tenant until she was 18. She then looked for employment:

> I did nannying jobs. It was the only thing I could do with Ruth. Mostly Americans. I'd always go to their house. If I'd have had my choice of work I'd have said no but because it was the only work I could do ... I done it well. I look after children very well. But it wasn't me, not at all.

Jane also trained as a beauty consultant and worked in a large chain store. She gave that job up because it involved working on Saturdays. She married and had a second child. At the time of the interview, she was living with her husband in a comfortable house that they own and jointly running a business from a computer base in the back room. The drive to succeed on her own and the need to provide for herself and Ruth has now been replaced by this joint venture, although she says she gets less satisfaction from the business.

Emma also had to forge a career without family members to help with child care. Emma was unusual in that she stayed on at the tuition unit to study at 'A' level. She has been determined to have a proper career and she applied to a large national company because they had a career structure. She wanted to start employment as soon as possible:

> Because I was getting, like old. If I went for a job at 21 they'd say we're going to pay you at a 16 year olds wage. That's the reason I went there. They have to pay you the going rate for your age.

Emma is also undertaking further study:

I'm doing a B.Tech. (Finance and Accounts). There's always a course to go to. It is good. I've got a staff board this week and if I get this promotion I shall be on £10,000–£13,000.

Her expressed motivation to work was partly 'boredom' and partly for her child. 'I'm doing all this for Sarah.' In fact she did have problems initially because the first childminder she used was not good and Emma found it hard going off to work and knowing that her daughter, then aged 2, was upset. Having found a new childminder, Sarah became very happy. Emma described this new childminder as being 'like a mum, like a grandma, like an aunty.' The cost of childminding has been such that there has been little if any financial benefit to her from working but she has a strong sense of the need to make the most of her life and looks to a future when financially she will be secure.

Those who didn't work mentioned the difficulties involved in earning enough to be the equivalent of benefits and the absence of good child care. On the whole it was seen as acceptable for a mother to look after her children while they were young but most felt they had little choice in any event.

The issue of age

> I've never seen how age is relevant but other people do. I can never see how someone can say, well you're only so and so, you can't do that. I mean, who says? (Wendy)

Age as an issue is a recurrent theme throughout for these mothers. A number of the young women spoke at length about the assumptions that had been made about them as mothers because of their age; they generated their own theories about the advantages and disadvantages of being young mothers. It is important to record these.

There was a general sense that young mothers were being looked down on:

> It was hard. Everyone kept looking down their nose at you, going ooh! All the time people would say 'That's a pretty baby, is that your brother?' They looked down their noses at me. (Kelly)

> I do get funny looks going up the road. (Barbara)

> It was highly embarrassing when I was pregnant to get on the bus and say 'Child's Fare please'. They looked at me and said 'Pardon?' (Tania)

As the children got older, it continued to be obvious that their mother was young:

> So many people don't think I'm so young. They ask me how old are you? I say 23, they say how old's your little girl, 7½, you can see them

112

calculating how old I was and the next question is ... ! They then ask so many questions. So many people are fascinated by the situation. (Jane)

When I mention I've got a little boy getting on for 8, they say you don't look old enough and I say, well I'm not. (Wendy)

To counteract a sense of implied criticism, some of the young mothers contrasted their experience with that of older mothers:

Now my friends are falling pregnant and this recession and that they're in the situation I was in eight years ago. My friend, she's like living in a hut and waiting to be rehoused. I feel really sorry for her now because when you're so young you think it's brilliant. You can handle it. You're not so mature and you don't think, Oh no! Having a room to myself and the baby was so much independence I couldn't ask for any more. (Jane)

I've got a friend now who is 28 and I met her in hospital. I mean, I knew everything but she hadn't got a clue. So some of these people that go about 'Bloody young mothers' they say, 'Don't got a clue about anything' and I say you should look at these older people – they haven't got a clue. I mean some young mothers there are, there's a girl lives up here who had a baby at 15 and she's never got the baby with her. You can get young people like that, you can get old people like that. Doesn't matter what age you are. (Annette)

Resentment of the prejudice against young mothers is at the heart of this debate. It was reflected earlier in Wendy's criticism of the gynaecologist:

I don't think he understood that you've got to judge each case on its own merits not on what you see before you.

Most mothers accepted that being a young mother was not something that they would recommend:

I wouldn't advise anyone that age to have a child because you're not ready for it. (Jane)

Reflecting on the experience they do pick up on certain advantages, such as having more patience or having the opportunity to have a career later. What Wendy says though is:

I wouldn't recommend it to anyone because it's an individual thing.

Once again it is Wendy who makes the point that individual young people may or may not be capable of meeting the challenge of motherhood:

No one ever believed I'd have children but I think that's a case of people adapt to their situation. Young people are not given enough credit for what they do. Until somebody's been there and done it ... I don't think they really understand.

113

13 Conclusion

Out of this material, there emerges a strong sense of these young women making their way through an obstacle course as they cope with the shock of the pregnancy, deal with the birth and establish themselves as mothers. Although there were experiences in common, it is the variety of experiences which is striking. At each stage they need to make a complex series of choices. Some issues appear to be beyond their control, such as the availability of housing, but even in those areas determination can overcome obstacles, so that a 16 year old has a council tenancy when theoretically this is not allowed.

The tuition unit's contribution was to treat the young mothers as adults and to enable them to take pride and pleasure in their babies while building their self-esteem as women.

The interviews were a very moving and inspiring glimpse into their lives. What it left was a feeling that these young mothers too should have the right to enjoy their babies and feel good about that experience. Being pleased to be a mother at fifteen may seem unlikely and even undesirable but welcoming the new baby and gaining self-esteem and satisfaction from caring for it is essential for the well-being of mother and baby. Attachments between two people can be formed at any age and stage. The attachment between a young mother and her baby need not be a problem if the mother is simply allowed to have the same feelings as older women.

Altogether the impression is of activity rather than passivity. These young women are fighters and survivors. They are undeniably disadvantaged by virtue of their early pregnancy and a number are disadvantaged by other circumstances also, such as conflict with parents and between parents, lack of educational achievement and poverty. In spite of this, the voices of these young women are not dejected and downtrodden. A sense of pride in what they have achieved, a sense of humour about their difficulties and a degree of wisdom about the pattern of their lives comes across very strongly.

Part III
ANALYSIS OF THE ISSUES: SOME PRACTICAL IMPLICATIONS FOR SERVICES

14 Themes

In Part III the ideas and material from the literature survey will be considered alongside the descriptions of the experience of pregnancy and motherhood given by the young women interviewed. This part will be divided into two broad sections: first, will be an analysis of the theoretical issues which emerged and some assessment of what has been learned; secondly, some conclusions will be drawn about the policy and practical implications of these findings. The first section will set out the tensions and contradictions which are inherent in the situation facing school age mothers. The second section will offer ideas for ways of dealing with these constructively in the provision of services.

Children as parents

It was possible to trace a line through very different literature sources that showed the centrality of the perceived tension between the child and the adult identity. As Murcott has summarised it:

> Child and adult are mutually exclusively conceptualised. It is impossible simultaneously to be adult and child ... Teenage pregnancy offends a morality which can identify children only by separating them from adults. (Murcott 1980 p. 7)

When interviewing young mothers for this research, it seemed that although circumstances, such as paying half fare on the bus, constantly reminded them that there were contradictions in their situation, they were on the whole able to live with that ambiguity and move between child and adult roles, expectations and needs. These moves would have occurred several times a day as they breastfed the baby before getting on with school work or negotiated with the housing department before resuming their dispute with a kid brother.

Although there were ambiguities arising from clearly identifiable 'adult' activities and 'child' activities, it seemed that much of their lives as children before becoming pregnant overlapped considerably with the adult world. Most had long-term boyfriends with whom they had a sexual relationship. Most spent a large part of their time out of the parental home, either at school or with friends. A number of them had experienced looking after younger siblings and cooking meals. Some had planned how they were to have a career or become a property owner and were working to achieve that end. So in terms of their day to day lives and in terms of their ideas about themselves, the transition to adulthood was a gradually occurring process which was already under way. Obvious though this may seem, it is an idea which is often missing from the literature on young mothers which seems to present the child/adult transition as being clear cut, like the age of consent, rather than as a gradual process of increasing maturity, such as is reflected in the Gillick ruling.

It was clear from the mothers that the accelerated move into adult roles before the age at which this is culturally the norm was not always easy. Some of them and their boyfriends did look back later and question whether they had missed out on some of the fun and freedom of teenage years. However, it would be wrong to assume that young mothers are incapacitated in their role as mothers because of this perceived loss. All first time mothers experience a sense of loss as well as a sense of gain, whether it be loss of career opportunities or loss of freedom, and for these girls, that loss took a particular form because of their age and stage. It is difficult to know whether there is a difference in the intensity as well as in the quality of this experience of loss. Perhaps an unplanned first pregnancy occurring to a successful career woman or an unplanned fifth pregnancy occurring at a point when a mother had returned to work after completing her family may match or even exceed the sense of loss experienced by a sixteen year old mother who had hoped to be a mother in her late teens or early twenties in any event.

This is not a particularly fruitful line to pursue – it is not, after all, a competition – however, it is necessary to draw attention to the potential for women at all stages in their lives to face stresses arising from their fertility. Women at all these crisis points need support to be offered uncritically and non-judgementally. Young women can cope with the demands of an adult role if given time and support which acknowledges their potential rather than making false assumptions about the divide between adults and children. As quoted earlier:

> I've never seen how age is relevant but other people do. I can never see how someone can say, Well, you're only so and so, you can't do that. I mean, who says? ... Young people are not given enough credit for what they do. (Wendy)

Separate or connected

One of the areas in which school age mothers move between child and adult roles is in their relationships with their families and in particular with their mothers. There is evidence that this is a normal experience in any first pregnancy, as Pines suggests:

> In particular, the relationship between the future mother and her own mother comes into the foreground; for the pregnant woman has to learn to play the role of mother to her unborn child whilst still remaining the child of her own mother. (Pines 1978 p. 21)

However normal this may seem, women who appear to remain too closely connected or indeed 'tied' to use the more common and more negative expression, to their mothers are deemed to have failed to achieve maturity. The fact that pregnant school girls and school age mothers are most likely to remain close to their mothers both emotionally and by living together is seen in the literature as one of the problems. This is to some extent because there is potential for conflict but more fundamentally because adults are said only to achieve an independent identity when they are fully separated from their parents. The research in this book certainly found that young mothers were most likely to return to their own parents or, if not, their boyfriend's parents, after the birth of the baby. Most were also likely to remain in close touch with their mothers and to continue to see them as a source of practical and emotional support for some time. The question is whether this limits their capacity to become responsible adults or demonstrates a lack of maturity.

The notion that maturity is associated with separateness has been challenged in recent years by women writers suggesting that this model is not appropriate for women. Gilligan (1982) drew on research into moral development to conclude that rather than achieving a mature identity through separateness, women often experienced an uninterrupted flow throughout their lives, in which their identity is defined in their relationships. She sees this as a source of strength in women.

These ideas have been seen as a radical contribution to the study of the development of women although as Nice (1992) points out, more than 30 years ago Young and Wilmott (1958) described the importance of the relationships which working class women sustained with their mothers. In her survey of the literature on mothers and daughters, Nice concludes:

> The overvaluing of autonomy and independence, 'going it alone' as a sign of adult status rather than the acceptance of our connection to others, has led to psychological theories which favour separation over connection and indeed insist on the young adult's separation from their family, and especially the daughter's separation from her mother, as a sign of the daughter's growth and healthy development. (Nice, 1992, p. 133)

In fact, the school age mothers in Ipswich did not appear to experience pressure to separate from their mothers and each tried to negotiate a degree of closeness which felt comfortable for them. Unfortunately the absence of a period of time when a girl is separate from the family is often perceived as part of the risk for the healthy development of the girl herself and as affecting her ability to mother her child.

Extending this argument further, it appears from the school age mothers interviewed that they gained satisfaction also from their relationship with their child. This is regularly pathologized in the literature, as described in Part I, as arising from the mother's own unmet needs, whereas an alternative model may suggest that the young mother's simultaneous close relationships with her own family and her baby provide a rich source of self-esteem and enable her to continue to develop. Although there can be obvious practical difficulties in the three generations living together, and it is rarely a permanent arrangement, the model of family life that emerges does have the potential for offering support at a critical time and does avoid some of the dangers of loneliness and isolation which first time mothers of any age can experience with a new baby.

Motherhood – dead end, ideal state or developmental process

If motherhood can be taken on by a child who is still maturing into adulthood and who continues to grow through her relationships, then motherhood should perhaps be seen as a state which permits development. This, however, is rarely acknowledged. Motherhood is more likely to be viewed as the end of a process, either an ideal state to be aspired to or a dead end to be avoided until freedom and a fulfilling career has been experienced. Although as Erikson (1980) describes it, motherhood may be seen as the culmination of adulthood and femininity, early motherhood is more often described as an experience of lost opportunities.

The contrast between young mothers and an idealised view of what life holds for other teenage girls lies behind many of the concerns in the literature. This viewpoint is graphically illustrated by Hudson and Ineichen in their description of a group of young mothers:

> Many were pale and anxious, puffing at a cigarette; some into their second or third pregnancies had a toddler crawling around their ankles. Their concerns, beyond their own health and that of their children, and whether or not hospital staff would be punitive in their approach, were centred on topics such as: will this week's giro (welfare payment) arrive safely? is my boyfriend really the father of my child? will he ever get a job? will my parents continue to tolerate me in our over-crowded council house when I have the baby? will I have to live in a high-rise flat, far from the area I grew up in, when it arrives? will it involve months of

120

living in a squalid bed and breakfast hotel first? (Hudson and Ineichen, 1991, p. 3)

The authors contrast this image with tall, healthy, secure, academically successful female medical students of the same age, preoccupied with such matters as social success in their hall of residence and conclude:

Differences in the long-term prospects of the two groups of young women do not need to be spelled out.

This contrast purports to be highlighting problems associated with teenage pregnancy and motherhood. It seems unlikely that they are implying that early motherhood prevented these young women from being tall, healthy and going to medical school. However it does describe the association between early motherhood and poverty in a way which suggests that their future is determined as much by the motherhood as by the poverty. The authors paint a dire picture in order to show concern for the difficulties many young mothers face. Unfortunately, they thereby contribute to the most negative of images of young mothers and give the impression that for them, motherhood is a source of unrelieved stress and anxiety. The material collected for this current research suggests a much more balanced picture in which young women can be seen as experiencing adversity but surviving it and at times achieving a sense of self-esteem to match those medical students. Fundamentally they see themselves as going through a process rather than being fixed for all time by the event of early motherhood.

If motherhood can be seen as a developmental process, then it is necessary to consider what areas of development are possible for very young women. There are two ways of approaching this: there is the possibility of motherhood in itself being a developmental process so that the role of mother and the experience of mothering are not static but allow for change and growth. At its simplest, for example, mothering a two year old is likely to have a different meaning, a different feel to it, from mothering an older child. However, age, personality and circumstances are likely to have an impact on that developing experience of motherhood so that the range of experiences is likely to change over time and will have different starting and finishing points. Halpin (1966) put it this way describing early motherhood:

We cannot just see it as an incident ... We have got to see it as a movement of growth in the direction of maturity.

Secondly the changing experiences of mothers will not only relate to the role and process of mothering but are bound to be tied up with how the women are changing and developing in other areas of their lives. However important the role of mother may be for many women, the other roles of partner, sister, friend, employee, employer also need to be negotiated over time.

121

So what do the experiences of very young mothers have to teach us about this process and does having a developmental perspective enable us to understand and perhaps help them through the experience? As described earlier, the young mothers who were interviewed initially dealt with being children and adults simultaneously. However that balance of roles gradually changed. During the initial phase of pregnancy and the early months of motherhood, they began to feel more comfortable with the role of mother and the responsibilities involved and undoubtedly there was development of the young mother's sense of self.

These early adaptations to the role took place within a social context of family, boyfriends, school, etc. As Part II demonstrated, the young women were very sensitive to the messages they received about such things as the morality of their decision to keep the baby and whether or not young women in general, and themselves in particular, could become competent mothers. Although most young women were fortunate enough to have some assistance from their families, most were also aware of their parents' distress that the situation had arisen and anxiety for their daughter's welfare. In this period of rapid changes, the role of the tuition unit was particularly helpful in providing positive messages about the young women's ability as adults to grow into motherhood while providing care and education for them as school children. As the young women described it, the unit helped them cope with the child/adult ambiguity and gave them hope. Handling this was probably easier outside the emotional intensity of family relationships but also outside the more traditional adult/child split within a school.

Subsequent adaptations within the role of mother are hard to separate from the other changes which the young women had to face. Again, this is usually seen as a problem. For example, how does a sixteen or seventeen year old cope with her feelings as a teenager and the care of her baby while moving into independent living? Although there are undeniably challenges involved in this, the young mothers themselves did not all seem to have experienced this phase as necessarily stressful. For some the stresses were balanced against the relief of being able to look after the child in the way they felt was best or being able to set up home with a boyfriend. There were stresses involved that arose from having to spend time in bed and breakfast accommodation or a poor quality homeless families unit. But most were able to see this as part of a process and looked back to their families for support and a day time base and forward to the prospect of having their own home at the end of it. Their familiarity with the likely pattern of events, gained from contact with other young mothers from the tuition unit, enabled them to cope with stressful conditions. (The use of homeless families units and bed and breakfast accommodation for young mothers must not be seen as desirable, however, and this will be mentioned later.)

Finally, by interviewing women in their early twenties who had given birth while still at school, it was possible to see that although having a baby when so young had seemed extraordinary and shocking at the time, it had become rather like any birth itself is for most women – an event that can be described in great detail and is clearly of significance but not one that currently could be said to dominate the way they saw their lives.

Reflecting on the way in which the young women described their experiences, it seems that life-span development theory (Sugarman 1986) has got a great deal to offer. The notion that development continues throughout the life-cycle has received increasing attention in recent years. As described in Part I, the research of Furstenberg (1987) into the long term outcomes for young mothers concluded that early pregnancy had certain consequences for young women in the short term but did not necessarily dictate the pattern of their lives in the long term. It is likely that changes and developments during the years of child care will vary according to other life choices which are made and to other circumstances, such as poverty and unemployment, which are beyond their control. The group studied in Ipswich varied considerably in the ways in which they balanced motherhood and career, independence and closeness to their parents etc. and the outcomes for themselves and their children will surely have depended to an extent on this balance. Equally, some mothers were able to leave their parents' home at a time of their choosing because housing was made available – others were not so fortunate.

It seems inevitable, therefore, that the notion of development as a mother will be a complicated product of personal strengths and resources influenced heavily by such varied matters as benefit systems and facilities available in the area where they live. The findings regarding young mothers in any particular area at any particular point in time can generate ideas about the range of possibilities and even identify some patterns but the lesson must be that only by knowing the circumstances of a particular group through careful enquiry and consultation, can a full understanding be gained of their situation and how they see their lives or potential to develop.

Negative stereotypes and the need for anti-discriminatory practice

The theme which has recurred throughout is the dominance of negative images of school age pregnancy and motherhood. Each time a social worker puts in a court report that the mother of a child is very young there is a danger that 'common sense views' will weigh this in the balance as a major risk factor in itself. As mentioned in the introduction, the current association with social problems and, by Government pronouncements, even disease contributes to what has become a common sense view of these young women as a problem to themselves, their children and society as a whole. Part I concluded with an analysis of why this might be so at an ideological level and Part II demonstrated how young women experienced some of those negative expectations and wanted to set the record straight. What Part II was also able to show was that such images fail to acknowledge the young women as individuals. The young mothers studied were able to accept the necessary contradiction here: none of them would suggest that becoming a mother while at school is a good idea or could possibly be recommended. Nevertheless they demanded the right to be treated with respect, to feel supported in their decision and to go about growing up and mothering in their own way. Using negative images as a way of perhaps frightening young women into giving up their babies for adoption or as a way of gaining resources leads to stigma and discriminatory attitudes.

The challenge for society therefore is how at the same time to acknowledge the difficulties and undesirability of pregnancy among very young women, providing education and contraceptive services, for example, so that they can feel in control of their own bodies, while at the same time enabling those who do become pregnant to make informed and independent decisions and to be supported with the outcome. These ideas are not contradictory if the model for understanding the issues and designing services is one of empowerment. Rutter's comment on resilience and coping with stress is useful here:

> Coping successfully with stress situations can be strengthening: throughout life, it is normal to have to meet challenges and overcome difficulties. The promotion of resilience does not lie in an avoidance of stress but rather in encountering stress at a time and in a way that allows self-confidence and social competence to increase through mastery and appropriate responsibility. (Rutter 1985)

In this sense, many dilemmas, such as making choices about sexual relationships in adolescence, can be seen as a potential source of stress. It would be unrealistic to anticipate that any form of secure family background or sex education is going to remove such stresses entirely. Therefore what is needed is not a model of intervention that singles out pregnancy or motherhood as isolated sources of stress but a model that builds on an understanding of the needs of adolescent girls to develop resilience and coping strategies. At each stage that is described in this research, issues arise which require the ability to make choices, master difficulties and take responsibility. From the study group we know that it is possible for even very young mothers to achieve that sense of mastery and indeed to feel a sense of pride that they did meet challenges and overcome difficulties. What they valued was a balance between special consideration and care because of their pregnancy and strongly expressed adult confidence in their ability to take responsibility, care for a child, pursue education and so on.

The mix of protecting and empowering children has been a major feature of the Children Act 1989. This is to be achieved by acknowledging the individual characteristics of each child, promoting all areas of development, valuing their relationships with their family and community and consulting their wishes and feelings. These basic principles fit comfortably with the messages from the study group and provide a good springboard for practical suggestions regarding the provision of services.

Before moving on, however, one final point must be made. The context in which many young mothers lived in the early stages was that of poverty. On the whole the provision of housing and availability of employment in Ipswich seemed better than is reported in other studies (e.g. Birch's study in Camberwell (1987)). Nevertheless the absence of proper benefits and available child care led to dependence on other family members and the pressure of living on very little money. It is important therefore to acknowledge that there are some sources of stress from which young mothers ought to be protected so that they can then be empowered to cope with the emotional and practical job of caring for their children successfully. All services must be seen in this context.

15 Services

Having identified some key ideas from the literature and from the experiences of the young mothers interviewed for this study, it is possible to draw some conclusions about what services might be seen as helpful. These conclusions will be framed predominantly in the form of the principles rather than the detailed practicalities of service provision. For convenience the need for services will be reviewed chronologically.

Sex education

Although as has become apparent from the literature and from the young women themselves, there is a complex relationship between knowledge about sexual relationships and the choices young women make, sex education in its broadest sense has to be seen as a fundamental starting point. Clearly knowledge of the mechanics of reproduction and contraception can never be seen as an adequate preparation for young women and of course young men, to enable them to cope with the physical and emotional changes they will experience as they reach puberty. The demand in the literature is for sex education to go beyond the scientific approach and deal with relationships. The message from young mothers would seem to confirm the need for sex education to become more comprehensive but also suggests that the language and style of presentation are equally important. As Wendy puts it:

> There's all sorts of pressures and when you're 14/15 you're not always thinking straight. Your hormones are up the chute anyway and they're sitting there saying 'and this is how this contraceptive works, this is what you must do and you mustn't do' – that's a load of crap ... You need to use slang words, not big words. Nobody knew until they tried it out what a messy, confusing business it can be. In the living and growing

programme it went on for hours. In reality, by the time you've said 'Ouch, get off' it's too late.

It is tempting to believe that there exists an ideal sex education programme which would meet the needs of all young people. However, on the basis of the conclusions in the literature and the views of the young women themselves, it is apparent that each young woman brings with her an individual set of experiences and attitudes. For some, information from school is extremely helpful, either in clarifying previous ideas or providing new knowledge which they have not gained from family and friends. For others, school may not be an appropriate forum to deal with such personal matters and the young people find it difficult to engage in any discussion. The gap in the system seems to be the lack of any private and confidential resource where young people can raise questions and dilemmas. Most of the young mothers had felt reluctance to discuss sexual relationships in any meaningful way with friends although joking about sex was frequent and there was an awareness that sexual relationships were commonplace. This sense of isolation may have been due to fear of the 'slag' label as Lees (1986) suggests, but it may be that young women are generally anxious about whether they are making the right choices and do not know where to turn for help.

Counselling services for young people are not well established in schools or in the community and certainly the young women in Ipswich didn't feel they had anywhere to turn for confidential advice. The Gillick ruling has paved the way for the idea that knowing that a girl under the age of 16 is having a sexual relationship can be kept confidential by General Practitioners in the interest of the health of the young woman. If young women are to be enabled to seek help as individuals rather than simply receive information by sitting in a class at school, then systems must be devised to ensure there is access to confidential counselling. It cannot be assumed that any one service can meet the needs of all young people and therefore a range of options must be available, both inside and outside the school system.

Availability of contraceptives

Use of contraception as has been established in Part I and Part II is affected by information, attitudes and availability. The interviews revealed great variation in all three elements. Although in this group there was no evidence of a deliberate plan to get pregnant, there was evidence that sustained use of contraceptives often required the commitment of both partners. The young women's ability to prevent a pregnancy depended on the availability of the pill, over which they had no control; the willingness of their boyfriend to use a condom, or their ability to refuse to have sex without a condom. In the era of AIDS awareness it could be said that this might encourage young women to engage in safer sex. It seems more appropriate to enable girls to take control of their fertility in the first instance since the risk of not using a condom might otherwise include an HIV positive young mother and baby.

As mentioned in Part I, the need for appropriate contraceptive services for young people has been linked with the Government's target of reducing the numbers of pregnancies under the age of 16 as has the need for improved sex education. However, there is no evidence that any one approach is the answer and until the Government accepts that young women are sexually active under the age of 16 and that resources have to be made available for services to be improved in all areas of education, contraception and counselling, young women will continue to be at risk of unplanned pregnancies.

Counselling in pregnancy

Whatever statistics are obtained to produce profiles of the typical school age pregnancy, individuals will continue to need a range of different resources to enable them to make decisions about the outcome of an unplanned pregnancy. For some this may simply mean a school accepting the mother's decision without criticism. For others, there are conflicts for her or conflicts within the family which may need help to resolve. The study group of mothers all felt positive about their decision to keep the baby at the time of the birth, but the process by which that decision was reached was not always an easy one and for some, an opportunity to discuss the matter with someone outside the family might have lessened their sense of isolation.

From an organisational point of view, it seems inevitable that counselling for young pregnant girls will need to be attached to an agency which also has other objectives – the number involved even in a town the size of Ipswich is still small. One possible choice would seem to be the contraceptive clinic and this form of counselling has been offered in other areas by Brook Clinics, for example. A second option may be that a counsellor attached to a tuition unit could provide a service. This is the option at the Arbour Project in Liverpool, although the counselling service there is to girls and their families and presupposes that the girls will have told their parents first.

For any counselling service to remain truly open-minded it must be possible for all outcomes to be seen in a positive light. As was discussed in Part I, the reasons offered by the literature for keeping the baby are alternatively seen as a result of social problems, i.e. if unemployment is your future, why not choose motherhood? or psychological problems, i.e. an emotionally deprived girl sees motherhood as acquiring a child to meet her needs. As Part II demonstrated, girls who chose to keep the baby were more likely to explain their choice in terms of a moral decision, i.e. it wasn't *right* to get rid of the baby through abortion or adoption. Their decision seemed to be a way of taking responsibility for what was seen as an unfortunate and undesired event, the pregnancy, and feeling a sense of obligation towards the child that had been created. Throughout the pregnancy, therefore, those girls who have decided to keep their baby must be allowed to feel that this is a positive choice and their decision respected. This has implications for all agencies involved.

The role of education

The debate in the literature about the usefulness of tuition units suggested that although they had advantages (e.g. Dawson 1987, Southwell 1985) they may be seen as isolating and stigmatising, (Miles 1979). Most young women interviewed who attended the tuition unit in Ipswich found that it enabled them to feel supported and gave them a much more positive view of themselves as young mothers. This enhanced their self-esteem and enabled them to face up to what they knew to be negative images in society in general. For some this was more important than for others. Where the family had been very supportive or where the school had been helpful and positive, that dependence on the unit seemed less. However, it was interesting that the unit was still seen very favourably by girls who had felt well supported by their family.

In considering the themes identified earlier in Part III, it seems that the unit was able to acknowledge the needs of the adult and the child in both challenging and supporting the young women. They were able to take a middle road between the 'ideal' and the 'dead end' views of motherhood, i.e. acknowledging the difficulties but enabling young women to recognise that they had the potential to be successful mothers. Alongside this was a clear message that they would continue to develop as young women as well as in their role as mothers.

There were two young women who felt either on education grounds or because they did not want to be seen as 'a problem' that they had not benefited greatly from attendance at the unit. Such views indicate the need for flexibility in the system. It may well be that from time to time individuals will want to stay within main stream school and this should be considered in a balanced way to see whether a more flexible package can be offered.

The lessons to be learned for those involved in planning the future of this unit or indeed those planning other tuition units, would seem to be the following:

1. Consultation with each girl is essential from the first contact to gain an accurate sense of how she sees her situation. She should have the opportunity to be seen on her own prior to being seen with her parents.

2. Acceptance is required of the fact that each individual will have a different set of needs and characteristics which must be accommodated in the education/support package which is provided. Each girl should participate fully in defining her own needs and planning a programme.

3. Flexibility is needed in the balance between the unit and other education resources. This appears to have increased recently at the unit in

Ipswich and acknowledges the need for some girls to have additional academic and social input from school or from specialist home tuition. Flexible use of the antenatal provision, perhaps to include girls who may have just left school, could also be a possibility.

4. Care needs to be given to all aspects of the progress of a young woman through the unit, from the time of the first referral to the need to offer aftercare. In Ipswich, the process within the unit appeared to be well planned but the time before and time after was rather variable.

5. Creche facilities need to be available close to the teaching rooms so that mothers can feel close to their babies but free of responsibility for them while they are studying.

6. Sensitivity is needed in the provision of emotional support. The balance between being supportive and being intrusive is a matter of personal style to some extent but where teachers are also put in the role of counsellors, they need to be offered opportunities for support and supervision for themselves. It may not be necessary for training as counsellors to be available but some consideration needs to be given to the skills required and the pressures involved in working with young women at such a critical time in their lives.

Inter-agency co-operation

A tuition unit cannot meet all the needs of all school age mothers and therefore should not function in isolation. It is important to find ways of ensuring that all agencies work together to provide appropriate responses from the point at which pregnancy is confirmed through to the child becoming a toddler and perhaps beyond. It may not be appropriate for an education resource to be the lead agency in this process but nevertheless the inter-agency implications need to be addressed in some form. It was suggested by the Joint Working Party report (Miles 1979) that the Community Health Service was appropriate as the lead agency. At present a tuition unit may be the only resource provided specifically for school age mothers. If that unit operates within a family centre then the potential for a longer term involvement and a wider brief exists but so also does the possibility of providing an impetus for linking education, social services, health and housing departments. The Local Authority under the Children Act (1989) has a duty to safeguard and promote the welfare of children who are in need (Section 17) and all agencies should contribute to this process. In these circumstances, both mother and child may be considered as in need of services.

The outcome of such inter-agency co-operation might be at the level of providing information to each young person about routes through the hospital system, the benefit system, the housing system etc. This could be particularly important for young mothers who are on their own after leaving the unit and need to know the resources in their area, such as other family centres, mother and toddler groups etc. It may also be possible for systems to be devised, for example, so that young mothers and their babies would not have to spend long periods of time in a homeless families unit or bed and breakfast accommodation without cooking facilities merely to show that they can pay rent consistently.

In general terms each agency must balance the needs of the young women to be treated as a 'normal mother', i.e. not discriminated against because of their age, while at the same time making provision for the fact that because they are young they may need extra help. For example, in hospital young mothers do not wish assumptions to be made about the likelihood that they will seek an abortion or to have their baby adopted. On the other hand, young mothers may be even more intimidated by the hospital system than older women and may need to be encouraged to state what they want; for example, to be asked whom they wish to be with them at the delivery of the baby. Young mothers do not require special treatment in all areas but some degree of sensitivity and understanding is necessary.

All agencies need to develop ways of acknowledging the role that families and boyfriends have to play. This is yet another difficult balance to achieve between working only with the young mother or appearing to leave the mother in a child role and relate to her parents. Again the answer must be to look to the young woman herself first. It can only be by fully engaging her that it will become possible then to offer appropriate support and information to the families and the fathers.

Finally, inter-agency co-operation may also be a way of monitoring the impact of factors, such as the benefits system, on young mothers. Unless there is a pooling of such concerns, this small group's interests risk being left in the hands of those who see them as a social problem.

131

16 Conclusion

Out of so many themes it seems invidious to select one above the others. However, there does appear to be a unifying factor which helps in analysing the issues, explaining the tensions between some of the literature and the experiences of this group of young mothers, and then looking towards developing more effective services. That factor is discussed explicitly in the research methodology for this project but is implicit in all parts of the debate. Young women who become pregnant while at school are not only discriminated against by virtue of their age, their sex and their pregnancy, but their accounts of their own experiences are too often discredited. The generation of negative stereotypes often appears to arise as a result of concern for what is deemed to be their plight but regularly reflects an unfortunate tendency to reinforce the stigma and prejudice which contributes to discriminatory attitudes. This is true of both literature and media coverage, although there are some notable exceptions.

The way forward is certainly not to deny the difficulties facing pregnant young women who decide to keep their babies; even the most happy and successful of young mothers did not recommend it as a choice. As this study has shown, young women need to be empowered to take control of their lives and those who become pregnant and become mothers need to be treated with respect and their voices heard.

Bibliography

Anderson, E.W., Kenna, J.C. and Hamilton, M.W. (1960), 'A Study of Extra-Marital Conception in Adolescence', *Psychiatria et Neurologia,* Vol. 139, No. 6.

Arbour Project (1990), Information Leaflet.

Berridge, D. and Cleaver, H. (1987), *Foster Home Breakdown,* Oxford: Blackwell.

Birch, D.M.L. (1987), *Are you my sister, Mummy?* London: Youth Support.

Boulton, M.G. (1983), *On Being a Mother: A Study of Women with Pre-school Children,* London: Tavistock.

Bowie, C. and Ford, N. (1989), 'Urban–rural variations in the level of heterosexual activity among young people', *Area,* Vol. 21 pp. 237–248.

Brown, G.W. and Harris, T. (1978), *The Social Origins of Depression,* London: Tavistock.

Bury, J. (1984), *Teenage Pregnancy in Britain,* London: Birth Control Trust.

Butcher, R.L. and Robinson, M.O. (1959), *The Unmarried Mother,* New York: Public Affairs Pamphlet No. 282.

Campbell, A.A., (1968), 'The role of family planning in the reduction of poverty: *Journal of Marriage and the Family,* Vol. 30 pp. 236–245.

Cant (1980), '"Can there ever be enough for me?" Reparenting the young single parent', *Journal of Adolescence,* 3, pp. 51–64.

Children Act (1989), HMSO.

Childright (1990), *Briefing on Gillick,* Children's Legal Centre.

Conger, J. (1979), *Adolescence – Generation Under Pressure,* Multimedia Publications.

Court Report (1976), *Fit for the Future.*

Coyne, A.M. (1986), *Schoolgirl Mothers,* Health Education Council.

Cunningham, A.M. (1984), *Teenage Pregnancy,* Pepar Publications.

Davies, P. (1983), 'Trapped: Unmarried West Indian Mothers in Handsworth', Papers on Community and Youth Work: Westhill College.

133

Dawson, N. (1987), *A Class of their own – study of Schoolgirl Pregnancy and Motherhood*, M.Ed. Thesis, Bristol University School of Education.

Dawson, N. (1989), 'Report on the 1987 Survey of Educational Provision for Pregnant School Girls and Schoolgirl Mothers in the Local Education Authorities of England and Wales', *Journal of Adolescent Health and Welfare* Vol. 2 No. 1.

Department of Health (1992), *The Health of the Nation.*

DES Circular No. 11/87, *Sex Education at School.*

Douglas, M. (1970), *Purity and Danger: an analysis of concepts of pollution and taboo,* Harmondsworth: Penguin.

Erikson, E. (1968), *Identity, Youth and Crisis,* New York: W.W. Norton & Co.

Erikson, E. (1980), *Identity and the Life Cycle,* New York: W.W. Norton & Co.

Estaugh, V. and Wheatley, J. (1990), *Family Planning and Family Well Being,* Occasional Paper No. 12, Family Policy Studies Centre and the Family Planning Association.

Evans, G. and Parker, P. (1985), 'Preparing Teenagers for Parenthood', *Midwives Chronicle and Nursing Notes.*

Farrell, C. (1978), *My Mother said,* London: Routledge and Kegan Paul.

Ford, N. (1988), *A survey of AIDS awareness and sexual behaviour and attitudes of young people in Somerset,* Institute of Population Studies, University of Essex.

Francome, F. (1983), 'Unwanted Pregnancies amongst Teenagers', *Journal of Biosocial Science,* Vol. 15 pp. 139–143.

Furstenberg, F.F., Brooks-Gunn, J., Morgan, S.P. (1987), *Adolescent Mothers in Later Life,* Cambridge: Cambridge U.P.

Gilligan, C. (1982), *In a Different Voice,* London: Harvard Press.

Griffin, C. (1985), *Typical Girls?* London: Routledge and Kegan Paul.

Halpin, H. (1966), *Pregnancy in Adolescence,* Report of a conference, National Council for the Unmarried Mother and her Child.

Howe, D., Sawbridge, P. and Hinings, D. (1992), *Half a Million Women,* London: Penguin.

Hudson, F. and Ineichen, B. (1991), *Taking It Lying Down,* London: Macmillan.

Ineichen, B., (1986), 'Contraceptive use and attitudes to motherhood among teenage mothers', *Journal of Biosocial Science,* 18, 4 pp. 387–94.

Jackson, S. (1982), *Childhood and Sexuality,* Oxford: Blackwell.

Jones, E.F., Forrest, J.D., Goldman, N., Henshaw, S.R., Lincoln, R., Rosoff, J.I., Westoff, C.F. and Wolf, D. (1985), 'Teenage Pregnancy in Developed Countries: Determinants and Policy Implications', *Family Planning Perspectives,* Vol. 17, No. 2.

Kendell, K. and Coleman, J. (1988), 'Adolescent Sexual Behaviour: The Challenge for Adults', *Children and Society,* Vol. 2. pp. 165–177.

Kiernan, K.E. (1980), 'Teenage Motherhood – Associated Factors and Consequences – The Experiences of a British Birth Cohort', *Journal of Biosocial Sciences,* Vol. 12, pp. 393–405.

134

Landy, S., Schiebert, J., Cleland, J.F., Clerk, C. and Montgomery, J.S. (1983), 'Teenage Pregnancy – Family Syndrome?' *Adolescence,* Vol. XVIII, No. 71, pp. 679–694.

Lees, S. (1986), *Losing Out,* London: Hutchinson.

McGrew, M.C., and Shore, W.B. (1991), 'Adolescent Pregnancy', *Journal of Family Practice*, Vol. 32, No. 1.

MacIntyre, S. (1977), *Single and Pregnant,* London: Groom Helm.

Malseed, J. (1987), 'Straw Men: A Note on Ann Oakley's Treatment of Textbook prescriptions for Interviewing', *Sociology*, Vol. 21, No. 4, pp. 629–631.

Melhuish, E. and Phoenix, A. (1987), 'Motherhood under twenty: prevailing ideologies and research', *Children and Society,* No. 4, pp. 288–298.

Mihill, C. (1992), 'Women at risk ignore safe sex', *The Guardian,* 5th May.

Miles, M., Bransmoll, M., Clarke, R., Cox, K., Hemming, J., Maxwell Bradley, C., Morrice, H., Smellie, E., Spicer, F. and Vincent, J., (1979), *Pregnant at School,* Report of the Joint Working Party on Pregnant Schoolgirls and Schoolgirl Mothers, London: National Council for One-Parent Families.

Miller, S.H. (1983), *Children as Parents,* London and New York: Child Welfare League of America.

Murcott, A. (1980), 'The Social Construction of Teenage Pregnancy: a Problem in the ideologies of childhood and reproduction', *Sociology of Health and Illness,* Vol. 2, No. 1, pp. 1–23.

Neustatter, A. (1986), *Mixed Feelings – The Experience of Abortion,* Pluto Press Ltd.

Nice, V. E. (1992), *Mothers and Daughters: The Distortion of a Relationship* London: Macmillan.

Oakley, A. (1979), *From Here to Maternity: Becoming a Mother,* Oxford: Martin Robertson.

Oakley, A. (1980), *Women confined,* Oxford: Martin Robertson.

Oakley, A. (1981), 'Interviewing Women' in Roberts, H. (ed), *Doing Feminist Research,* London: Routledge and Kegan Paul.

OPCS, *Trends in conceptions and terminations and maternities 1969–1989.*

Osofsky, J.J., Osofsky, J.D., Kendall, N. and Rejan, R. (1973), 'Adolescents as Mothers: An Interdisciplinary Approach to a Complex Problem', *Journal of Youth and Adolescence,* Vol. 2, No. 3.2.

Phoenix, A. (1991a), *Young Mothers?* Cambridge: Polity Press in association with Basil Blackwell.

Phoenix, A. (1991b), 'Mothers under Twenty: Outsider and Insider Views', in Phoenix, A., Woollett., A. and Lloyd, E. (eds), *Motherhood,* London: Sage.

Phoenix, A., Woollett, A. and Lloyd, E. (eds), (1991), *Motherhood,* London: Sage.

Phoenix, A., and Woollett, A. (1991), 'Motherhood: Social Construction, Politics and Psychology', in Phoenix, A., Woollett, A. and Lloyd, E. (eds), *Motherhood* London: Sage.

Piaget, J. (1954), *The Origins of Intelligence in Children,* New York: International Universities Press.

Pines, D. (1978), 'On Becoming a Parent', *Journal of Child Psychotherapy,* Vol. 4, No. 4.

Quinton, D., and Rutter, M., (1988), *Parenting Breakdown; The Making and Breaking of Intergenerational Links,* London: Avebury.

Rayner, E. (1971), *Human Development,* London: Allen and Unwin.

Ribbens, J. (1989), 'Interviewing – An "Unnatural Situation"?' *Women's Studies Int. Forum,* Vol. 12, No. 6, pp. 579–592, USA.

Richman, N. (1978), 'Depression in mothers of young children', *Journal of the Royal Society of Medicine,* Vol. 71, pp. 489–93.

Roberts, H. (1981), *Doing Feminist Research,* London: Routledge and Kegan Paul.

Russell, J.K. (1982), *Early Teenage Pregnancy,* Edinburgh: Churchill Livingstone.

Rutter, M. (1985), 'Resilience in the Face of Adversity,' *British Journal of Psychiatry,* Vol. 147.

Schofield, M. (1968), *The Sexual Behaviour of Young People,* Harmondsworth: Penguin.

Shaffer, D., Pettigrew, A., Wolkind S. and Zajicek, E. (1978), 'Psychiatric aspects of pregnancy in schoolgirls: A review', *Psychological Medicine,* 8. pp. 119–130.

Sharpe, S. (1987), *Falling for Love: Teenage Mothers Talk,* London: Virago.

Simms, M. and Smith, C. (1986), *Teenage Mothers and Their Partners,* London: HMSO.

Skevington, S., and Baker, D. (eds) (1989), *The Social Identity of Women,* London: Sage.

Smith, K. (1989), 'Two by Two – Babes in Class', *The Times Scottish Educational Supplement* 1.12.89.

Smith, K. (1990), 'Class room for mothers', *The Guardian* 26.6.90.

Southwell, M. (1985), *Pregnancy, Maternity and Education,* National Council for One-parent Families.

Spender, D. and Sarah, E. (1980), *Learning to Love,* The Women's Press Limited.

Steen, E. (1990), 'Has child sex reached the age of consent?' *The Independent on Sunday,* 18.11.90.

Strauss, A. (1987), *Qualitative Analysis for Social Scientists,* Cambridge: Cambridge University Press.

Sugarman, L. (1986), *Life Span Development,* London: Methuen.

Sukanich, M.D., Awapin, C., Rogers, M.D., Kenneth, D., McDonald, M.D. and Hugh, M. (1986), 'Physical Maturity and Outcome of Pregnancy in Primiparas Younger than 16 years of age', *Paediatrics,* Vol. 78, No. 1.

Thoburn, J., Murdoch, A., and O'Brien, A. (1986), *Permanence in Child Care,* London: Blackwell.

Voydanoff, P. and Donnelly, B.W. (1990), *Adolescent Sexuality and Pregnancy*, USA: Sage.

Wilkinson, S. (ed.), (1986), *Feminist Social Psychology: Developing Theory and Practice*, Milton Keynes: O.U. Press.

Wilson, Fiona (1980), 'Antecedents of Adolescent Pregnancy', *Journal of Biosocial Science*, 12, 141–152.

Wolkind, S.N. and Kouk, S. (1985), 'Teenage pregnancy and motherhood', *Journal of the Royal Society of Medicine*, Vol. 78.

Woollett, A. (1991), 'Having Children: Accounts of Childless Women and Women with Reproductive Problems' in Phoenix, A., Woollett, A. and Lloyd, E. (eds), *Motherhood* London: Sage.

Zongker, C.E. (1977), The Self-Concept of Pregnant Adolescent Girls, *Adolescence*, Vol. XII, No. 48.